W9-BON-326

A Guide to
College Life

Student to Student
Written by College Students • Compiled by Paul Buchanan & Paula Miller

Regal

From Gospel Light
Ventura, California, U.S.A.

Published by Regal
From Gospel Light
Ventura, California, U.S.A.
www.regalbooks.com
Printed in the U.S.A.

Library of Congress Cataloging-in-Publication Data
Student to student : a guide to college life / compiled and edited by Paula Miller, Paul Buchanan.
p. cm.
ISBN 978-0-8307-4538-8 (trade paper)
1. Christian college students—Religious life. 2. Christian college students—Conduct of life. I. Miller, Paula Jean. II. Buchanan, Paul, 1959-
BV4531.3.S78 2007
248.8'34—dc22
2007021803

3   4   5   6   7   8   9   10   11   12   13   14   15   /   17   16   15   14   13   12   11   10

Rights for publishing this book outside the U.S.A. or in non-English languages are administered by Gospel Light Worldwide, an international not-for-profit ministry. For additional information, please visit www.glww.org, email info@glww.org, or write to Gospel Light Worldwide, 1957 Eastman Avenue, Ventura, CA 93003, U.S.A.

Contents

A Note from the Compilers

As professors, we sometimes like to think of ourselves as fonts of knowledge from whom you, our eager students, learn things of great importance—but who are we kidding? Deep down we know that is seldom the case. (We were students ourselves once, and we remember!)

College students learn much more about life—about heartbreak and joy, loyalty and faith—from each other than they ever do from us. When it comes to teaching life lessons, our class lectures and PowerPoint presentations will never rival cafeteria debates, post-date recaps or late-night burger runs.

That's why *Student to Student: A Guide to College Life* is written by Christian college students from across the country. Here are their collected stories about experiences that have helped shape the adults they are becoming, and about the real everyday challenges, temptations and moments of grace in the world of higher education.

We hope this book will encourage you in the midst of your hectic lives. More importantly, though, we hope these sometimes funny, sometimes poignant stories from your peers will resonate with you and cheer you and remind you what is truly essential in this busy, formative season of your life.

God bless,
Paula Miller
Paul Buchanan

An Exercise of the Mind

Taking Our Thoughts Captive

By Hillary Prag, Seattle Pacific University

Don't copy the behavior and customs of this world, but let God transform you into a new person by changing the way you think.
ROMANS 12:2, *NLT*

I have decided that my athletic abilities are a disgrace to my father. When my dad was in his late 30s, he raced in an Ironman triathlon after training nonstop for a year with a former Ironman champion. The race took 12 hours, and I was tired from just standing and clapping for him all day.

Currently my best efforts at physical fitness involve a morning walk-run. I pride myself in being able to jog up a very steep and strenuous hill in my neighborhood. It's about 10 steps long. That's pretty much the extent of my jogging, because afterward I'm so winded that I have to stagger along the rest of the route. I tend to avoid eye contact with the neighbor lady walking her twin Scottish terriers at this point. Yet without this humiliating routine, my day cannot begin. It is somehow comforting to me.

The reason I'm calmed by my sad attempt at exercise is because I spend this time organizing my waking brain. Jogging in the morning helps me focus the thoughts that flop around in my mind like laundry in a dryer. I'm worried about a broken friendship, my family in a foreign country, homework that probably won't get done today, and the meeting I must plan for next week. I stop to catch my breath. It occurs to me to focus on exercising my body for a few minutes. I have to turn off the dryer to do this.

To get to the place where we can be completely present in the moment, we must learn to take our thoughts captive. This process happens when we turn off the tumbling dryer, carry all the loose socks, shirts and towels to the foot of the Cross and dump them there for a while. Once we've done that, then we can rest from our concerns and live freely in the present moment. (But usually, we drop a sock or two and have to go back, pick it up and bring it to the pile.)

However you visualize the unruly activity in your mind, know that you can have control over it through the Holy Spirit. He is our Counselor and will guide us in what we think. There is a famous prayer that says, "God grant me the serenity to accept the things I cannot change, the courage to change the things I can and the wisdom to know the difference." Trust the Holy Spirit to give you the wisdom to know the difference today.

My mind is a bad neighborhood that I try not to go into alone.
ANNE LAMOTT

Wisdom for the Week

DAY 1: 1 CORINTHIANS 9:24-27

DAY 2: PHILIPPIANS 3:13-21

DAY 3: EPHESIANS 4:22-30

DAY 4: GALATIANS 6:12-18

DAY 5: ISAIAH 62:1-10

Staying Fit

- Join an intramural team, even if you're not particularly good at the sport. You'll increase your physical activity and make new friends.

- Enroll in a physical education class that teaches a skill you don't already practice, like karate, tennis, Pilates or swimming.

- Take a college aerobics class for credit, and learn your way to a healthy lifestyle.

- Go to the campus fitness center, and develop the habit of working out each week.

- Find a fitness buddy who'll work out with you and hold you accountable.

- Find some good exercise videos, and do the routines alone or with others in your dorm or apartment.

- Exercise at least three days each week, but vary your routine: bike, swim, run, jog or just walk briskly.

- Stretch to keep muscles and joints limber before and after exercise.

2

Me: The Anti-Conflict

Learning to Love Head-On

By Elizabeth Kay York, Whitworth College

Do not suppose that I have come to bring peace to the earth.
I did not come to bring peace, but a sword.

MATTHEW 10:34

The summer that I worked as a camp counselor in the majestic evergreen-covered mountains of Colorado, I came up against several obstacles. Freezing tents and cabins, a forest fire that caused a temporary evacuation, and my chronic homesickness were all unexpected complications of that summer in the forest—which I had eagerly anticipated. Yet above all these impediments to a perfect summer, my own fear was the largest obstacle. Each week when the busloads of new campers arrived, I feared what they would think of me. Was I adequate for the job? Did I have the right personality? I especially feared any conflict that would require me to confront my campers. I wanted a smoothly paved summer ride with no bumps or ruts in the road.

During weeks three and four, the camp was without campers due to a fire that ravaged the forest but thankfully did not touch the camp. During that time, I read a book about evangelism. I was deeply impressed with its idea that Jesus was *not* an appeaser. When the rich young man asked Christ about how he could enter the kingdom of heaven, Jesus told him frankly what he must do (see Matthew 19:16-22). Jesus did not change Himself to draw the man to His side. As gentle as He was, Jesus never bent His teachings or His character to impress others. He faced people down when the situation called for confrontation. Convicted, I asked God to forgive my sin of people-pleasing and pleaded that He would change me.

Two weeks later, I had a week of conflict like never before. On the first bright day of camp that week, one of my campers stole a tent-mate's shoes. For days, there was incessant gossip, quarrelling and grudge holding among my seven campers. They were angry at each other and indifferent to me. Before that week, I would have tried to cover over the problems and minimize their significance. But I had changed because of the example of Christ. Instead of ignoring the problems, I faced them head-on. I encouraged apologies and instructed the girls about how I expected them to treat each other lovingly. By the end of the week, the girls were a unified group. I was delighted to see them laughing together and building one another up. To my surprise, they admired me for gently yet firmly prodding them.

My fear of conflict had been just that—a fear. I learned that avoiding conflicts in dread of others' reactions is not love. My focus on what the campers would think of me only stunted relationships and spiritual progress. When I focused instead on loving God and them, even conflicts turned bright for His glory.

> *Fear of man will prove to be a snare, but whoever*
> *trusts in the Lord is kept safe.*
> PROVERBS 29:25

Wisdom for the Week

DAY 1: 2 TIMOTHY 1:3-10

DAY 2: MATTHEW 22:43-45

DAY 3: JOHN 12:37-47; ACTS 1:8-14

DAY 4: ROMANS 8:26-31; PSALM 73:24-28

DAY 5: 2 THESSALONIANS 3:1-5; JUDE 17-25

Tips for Conflict Resolution

- When conflicts arise, encourage everyone involved to share their opinions.

- Listen carefully to all sides.

- Acknowledge that it takes courage to voice one's opinion.

- Expect dissension without becoming defensive. Admit mistakes.

- Foster an environment of mutual respect; curtail personal attacks.

- Promote problem solving among the group members in conflict.

- Highlight areas of agreement; find common ground.

- Establish clear expectations for resolution.

- Face the conflict rather than avoid it; aim for a solution rather than a withdrawal.

3

Do You Not Perceive It?

Being Alert for What God Has in Store

By Matthew Castle, Azusa Pacific University

See, I am doing a new thing! Now it springs up; do you not perceive it?
I am making a way in the desert and streams in the wasteland.
ISAIAH 43:19

I climbed out of the back of the muddy SUV, and I could feel my muscles stretch and thank me for releasing them from the captivity of the vehicle. We were on a summer mission trip in the country of Chile in South America, and had been driving nearly six hours. We were now stopped at a turnout on a long and winding road up into the Andes Mountains, and as we approached the edge of the mountain, our jaws dropped in amazement. We were overlooking the entire Santa Barbara Valley and could see miles of rural villages and farmland all around.

Our leader told us about the valley and about the things God was doing there. He explained that the people in these villages were very poor and lived off whatever food they managed to grow on their own farms, and that there were only about 10 known Christians in the entire 300-square-mile valley. Before we had a chance to feel disheartened, he told us about the three churches that were being planted in the area and the specific ministries each was going to have. We paused and prayed over that valley and then reluctantly climbed back into our cars. But

I will never forget that view. God is doing great things there because of a handful of people who are sensitive to His leading.

Upon returning to the United States, I've thought of that experience often. There is so much need in the world, and it sometimes seems like one individual can do so little. Yet God is using that scattering of believers in that huge valley to do so much. So I often find myself wondering, *What is the "Santa Barbara Valley" in my life? Is God trying to show me or lead me to something new? Is He beginning a great work, even with people as limited as I am?* God is calling you and me to look toward the future. What is it that He is preparing us to do?

Wisdom for the Week

DAY 1: COLOSSIANS 1:9-12;
        MARK 11:20-24
DAY 2: ROMANS 1:8-17
DAY 3: 2 PETER 1:2-12
DAY 4: 1 TIMOTHY 1:7-11
DAY 5: MATTHEW 4:18-22

Mission: Possible

Many missions agencies welcome college students to take part in short-term missions. If you attend a Christian college, there might be a student association at your school that can help you explore some spring break or summer short-term mission opportunities. If you go to a secular school, there will likely be a Christian student association on campus, such as Campus Life, that might be able to provide you with similar resources.

Here are some Internet sources that might aid your exploration of short-term mission opportunities:

- The Association of Gospel Rescue Missions (AGRM): www.agrm.org.
- Adventures In Missions (AIM): www.adventures.org.
- Mission Trips Inc. (MTI): www.missiontrips.com.
- Short Term Missions: www. ShortTermMissions.com.
- United States International Ministries Group (USIMG): www.usimg.org.

Here are some books that might help you determine if short-term missions are right for you:

- *Before You Pack Your Bag, Prepare Your Heart* by Cindy Judge (Wheaton, IL: Campfire Resources, 2000).

- *Building Credible Multicultural Teams* by Lianne Roembke (Pasadena, CA: William Carey Library, 2000).

- *Essential Guide to the Short-term Mission Trip* by David C. Forward (Chicago: Moody Press, 1998).

- *A Guide to Short Term Missions* by H. Leon Greene (Portland, OR: Gabriel Publishing, 2003).

- *Turkey: The Lost Land of the Bible* by Andrew Jackson (Colorado Springs, CO: World Christian News and Books, 2003).

- *Mack and Leeann's Guide to Short-Term Missions* by J. Mack and Leeann Stiles (Downers Grove, IL: InterVarsity Press, 2000).

The Hug

Loving a Hurting Child

By Kylie McCuen, University of California, Santa Barbara

We know that we have passed from death to life, because we love our brothers. Anyone who does not love remains in death.

1 JOHN 3:14

This Fourth of July was going to be unlike years previous. Instead of watching fireworks at the park, I was going to spend Independence Day with 60 fourth-grade, fifth-grade and sixth-grade kids from all over Southern California at a church camp in the mountains. I had attended this camp for years, and now, being 19 and having just finished my freshman year, I was finally going back as a counselor.

Camp lasted a week, and the Fourth of July fell on Friday. While planning the various activities for the campers, we counselors decided to have a carnival after dinner to celebrate the holiday. The carnival was a blast! We had a sponge-toss, snow cones, three-legged races and all the other activities I associate with the Fourth—everything but fireworks. However, what made that day stand out in my memory—what nearly brought me to tears—was a simple hug. That hug came from a little boy I'll call Peter.

For Peter, the camp was a respite from the emotional scars created by his bleak life with drug-addicted, unloving parents. When I first heard about Peter's living situation, I made it my mission to fill his time at camp with the love and security he seldom enjoyed. It was hard at first because Peter was almost dead to love. If I set my hand on his shoulder as a gesture of congratulations or reassurance, Peter pulled way. If I saw him sitting by himself on the couch and joined him, he would automatically scoot farther down.

But I kept it up. I was gentle and persistent, and my resolve began to pay off. Eventually, Peter didn't jerk away when I touched him—he actually came and sat by me. On the night of the Fourth of July festival, Peter won the Water-Gun Showdown, and when he did, he ran directly to me and threw his thin arms around my neck in a spontaneous hug. Who knew how long it had been since he had hugged anyone?

I knew in that moment that I had shown Peter enough persistent love that he could finally reciprocate affection. Peter had become alive with love, and by the time the buses arrived on Sunday to take the campers home, he was hugging the other counselors as well.

I lost contact with Peter once I went back to school, but I often think about him. I hope that the Peter I saw blossom at camp did not wither into a half-life of neglect. I hope Peter lives a life of love.

Wisdom for the Week

DAY 1: 1 CORINTHIANS 9:19-23

DAY 2: MARK 6:34-44

DAY 3: 1 CORINTHIANS 3:9-11

DAY 4: MARK 8:34-48

DAY 5: LUKE 14:12-14

How to Have a Great Fourth of July Celebration

Do . . .

- Observe the celebration of American liberty. Hang out the stars and stripes.
- Barbecue. Grill burgers so tasty that even your vegetarian neighbor will be envious.
- Heed safety instructions before lighting fireworks. Everything's fun and games until somebody loses a finger. Have a fire extinguisher handy.
- Watch a parade. Clap loudly and often, and cheer for every armed forces group that marches by.
- Enjoy the day with friends and relatives. Bear in mind that familiar adage: The family that sweats together, sticks together.

Don't . . .

- Don't use fireworks at all if they're illegal in your area.
- Don't set off fireworks near anything flammable, including dry grass (common in July!) or buildings of any kind.
- Don't light giant sparklers with a short match unless you like the look of singed eyebrows.
- Don't inhale if you set off smoke bombs.
- Don't volunteer to be the pool monitor for the 20 grade-school cousins playing in the backyard pool (unless you're an education major, and even then, it's risky).

—Todd A. Miller, Biola University

The College Lost and Found

Pursuing Christ and Finding Myself

By Karen Porter, Yale University

*"For I know the plans I have for you," declares the LORD, "plans to prosper
you and not to harm you, plans to give you hope and a future. Then you
will call upon me and come and pray to me, and I will listen to you.
You will seek me and find me when you seek me with all your heart."*

JEREMIAH 29:11-13

Rifling through stacks of résumés and half a dozen unfinished
job applications, I was searching for . . . something. What was
it? Sighing, I shook my head. *You're beginning to lose it, Karen.*

What had happened? College was supposed to be about
"finding myself": discovering my passion, embracing my purpose, finding my place in the world. Why then, after three and
a half years of immersing myself wholeheartedly in the university experience—dedicating myself to intense academic studies, sampling a smorgasbord of extracurriculars, even going to
church and growing in godly fellowship—did I feel more *lost*
than *found*?

I wanted desperately to hear God's call, to know His specific plan for my life. For three years, I had agonized over every decision: selecting the perfect major, striking the perfect balance
between people and academics, and now finding the perfect
career. Not quite sure what I was looking for, I had rummaged

through the "Lost and Found" of life, trying on a hundred different hats—two universities, four majors and countless clubs. Yet passion and purpose remained elusive.

"God," I prayed, "I am trying so hard—*so* hard. Why can't I find my calling?" Then it hit me: *I* was trying. *I* was striving. Was the revelation of God's plan really dependent on *me* and *my* effort?

In Jeremiah 29, God reassured the Israelites in exile with His promise of a plan for "hope and a future." God's plan, however, wasn't dependent on the Israelites' determining each and every detail; indeed, nothing suggests that He intended to reveal it fully in advance. Simply, God called His people to faithfully pursue Him, and He promised to take care of the rest.

I suddenly realized that I had been striving for the wrong thing. Relying on my own effort, I had fought to figure out God's plan, yet failed to get to know the Person behind it. I had sought precise details and strove for perfection when God simply called me to seek Christ. College *was* about finding myself: lost in this world . . . and found in Christ.

As pilgrims in progress, we may not always know His plan—
but we can trust Him with the process.

Wisdom for the Week

Day 1: Psalm 9:7-10

Day 2: Psalm 34:1-8

Day 3: Psalm 40:1-5

Day 4: Habakkuk 3:17-19

Day 5: Acts 27:15-25

What's My Calling?

Many Christian students seem to be waiting for their personally addressed manila envelope containing God's plan for their lives. They pray for it daily and put decisions on hold, waiting to hear God's calling. Christian colleges, like the one I attend, seem to be teeming with students who won't even choose what color pen to use without praying over the decision.

Sometimes we get scared to make decisions, fearing we will choose something outside God's calling. We pass up job opportunities or internships because we're worried they won't contribute to some future goal. We pass up ministry opportunities with the homeless or with the elderly, believing we have not felt God's direction.

But is it possible these missed opportunities could have opened our eyes to a need or taught us to love someone different from ourselves? Could God have used us in a ministry we didn't feel directly called to?

Few Christians discover one single calling. Many of us are called to various things at different points in our lives, and God uses each experience to teach us more about Him. But there *is* one call God has for every Christian: to serve Him and further His kingdom.

If we make choices that give us occasion to fulfill that purpose, we should never fear that we have chosen something outside God's calling.

—Sara Highhouse, Biola University

Miracles Are No Myth

Experiencing the Hand of God

By Jeff Arnold, Biola University

He said: "The LORD is my rock, my fortress and my deliverer;
my God is my rock, in whom I take refuge, my shelf and
the horn of my salvation."
2 SAMUEL 22:2-3

When I was five years old, my father, a professor, took a sab-
batical and my family moved to Germany for nine months. We
lived in a very low-rent apartment, but it was on the edge of a
forest—much to my delight. Even better, it was near a beautiful
pond full of all kinds of wildlife.

The road that led through the forest from our apartment
went down a steep hill. At the bottom of the slope was my
beloved pond. My mom took us there as often as she could. She
would push my two-year-old brother in his stroller, and I would
walk along beside them, doing my best to keep up. On one of
our trips down the hill, my legs started to ache from all the
walking we'd done, and I begged for a turn in the stroller. My
brother didn't mind walking for a while, so he and I swapped
places—I buckled myself in, and he ambled behind.

I was rolling along in my seat, enjoying my leisurely ride,
when I heard my brother scream. I looked back to see him
lying on his face on the pathway, screaming in a panic for our

mother. He'd apparently tripped and done a face-plant on the pavement. My mom, being a loving parent, hurried back to tend to her crying toddler.

In her concern for her second-born son, she overlooked one thing: She rushed to his rescue so quickly that she forgot to set the brake on the stroller. I clung to the stroller seat and headed downhill, picking up speed like a soapbox racer.

At the bottom of the path was a river embankment—a good 30-foot drop—and my freewheeling stroller zoomed straight for it. I don't remember if I screamed or if my terror robbed me of the power of speech, but I clearly remember looking back and seeing my mother, who had abandoned her other screaming youngster to sprint after me, just as the stroller reached the edge of the road and headed across the gravel toward the embankment.

The next logical thing would have been for the stroller to launch off the edge of the embankment into the riverbed below—but instead, it slowed to a halt. Flushed with adrenaline, I looked around. There was nothing there to stop me—no trees, no bushes, no rocks. The brakes had not magically locked in place. The stroller simply stopped right at the very moment I was closest to perishing. My mother caught up to me, pulled me from the stroller and hugged me, crying, until all of us could catch our breaths and steady our nerves.

When any of our family members tell this story, we have only one possible explanation for what happened that day: The Lord our God chose to keep me alive. Now any time I cry out for help to the One who loves me more than I can possibly imagine, I remember that day. The same God who reached down to stop my careening stroller can intervene again in my life, in ways I can never comprehend or foresee!

Wisdom for the Week

DAY 1: EXODUS 15:1-2

DAY 2: PSALM 37:38-39

DAY 3: ACTS 13:44-48

DAY 4: ISAIAH 12:1-3

DAY 5: 1 THESSALONIANS 2:15-17

Everyone Remain Calm!

It can be a risky world out there, so here are a few survival tips that might come in handy:

- *How to survive if you are in an earthquake:* If you're inside, stand in a doorway or crawl under a desk or table. Stay away from windows and unanchored bookcases or shelves. If you're outside, stay away from buildings, trees and power lines. Turn on a radio for emergency instructions.

- *How to survive if you are attacked by a bear:* If you can't get away, climb up a tree (higher than the bear can climb!). If there are no trees, face the bear, hold up your arms or open your jacket—anything that will make you look bigger. If this doesn't stop the bear, lie down, cover your head and play dead.

- *How to survive if you're in a Hitchcock movie:* Drive past all those no-name motels until you see a Best Western. Always take baths. Don't climb high spiral staircases or tall buildings. If violins start playing, run. If you're blonde and female, consider one of Clairol's many fine hair-coloring products. Never drink glowing milk.

—Heather Buchanan, Chapman University

Never Alone

Trusting the Presence of God

By Anya Eckelbarger, Anderson University

*Since God assured us, "I'll never let you down, never walk off
and leave you," we can boldly quote, "God is there, ready to help;
I'm fearless no matter what. Who or what can get to me?"*
HEBREWS 13:5-6, *THE MESSAGE*

A day and a half after stepping on a plane, my feet were planted
on the solid ground of the city I would eventually grow to love
as home. It had only been two days since my family left our
cozy house in Michigan to journey to the former Soviet Union.
My parents, both pastors, had felt a strong connection with the
story of the Russian people. So after prayer and discussion, we
began our missionary journey into a land whose communist
system and way of life had fallen apart only three years earlier
and left its people in ruin.

As we entered the airport terminal, which was constructed
of miles of marble and iron, my eight-year-old frame felt very
small. I was struck by my insignificance as I walked past
machine-gun-wielding guards who yelled at us in a foreign (to
me, anyway) tongue. Unsure of what lay ahead, I squeezed my
mother's hand; fear pushed every thought from my mind.
Suddenly my mother was pushed backward and commanded
to halt. There we stopped. A red line on the floor was all that

separated us from the end of our travel and the beginning of our journey.

My mother passed ahead of me through the customs line, having been waved through by the burly, annoyed man behind the counter. I was at the front of the line now, the only one in the family who had not crossed over. At my young age, all I sensed was that this angry man held my fate in his hands. If he let me pass, I would be safe with my family. If he stopped me, I would be taken away. *Should I risk it or run back to safety in America? Stay with me, God,* I prayed as I took my first step past fear.

Those moments when I waited to cross the border felt like hours. Finally, the officer waved me over and placed the precious green-leather passport back in my small hand. My mind cleared as I thought, *Welcome to Moscow!*

I remain amazed at how God has touched my life and stayed with me through every fearful experience. On that terrifying day, I began to recognize that Christ overcomes all fear. God stood with me. He heard my childish plea for protection. He used our journey across the ocean for a bigger purpose. I learned on that day that with God's presence, every experience is a time of strength and learning, without reason to fear.

Wisdom for the Week

DAY 1: PSALM 5:11-12

DAY 2: PSALM 61:1-6

DAY 3: ISAIAH 25:4-8

DAY 4: 1 CORINTHIANS 16:13-14

DAY 5: DEUTERONOMY 12:10-12

Out of the Zone

Sometimes being God's servant means getting outside our comfort zones. If it feels like God is calling you to do something you find intimidating, here are a few things to keep in mind:

- **It gets easier every time.** Whether it's singing in front of a packed auditorium or standing up for what you believe, nothing lessens fear like experience. If you go out on that limb the first time, it will be much easier the second.

- **If at first . . .** It's easy to measure things in terms of success and failure, but when it comes to getting out of our comfort zone, it might be better to think in terms of progress and growth. Don't expect an immediate triumph. Remember: Moses' first meeting with Pharaoh wasn't such a huge success either.

- **There aren't any tricks**. Quick fixes just don't work. You may not look down, but you *still* know you're a long way off the ground. And do any of us actually want to picture our audience in its underwear? There aren't really any shortcuts when it comes to going outside the zone. Fear is fear, and the best way to overcome it is to face it.

- **God's got your back.** We hear it over and over again. We say it to each other constantly. It's in the books we read and the sermons we hear. But it really *is* true: God *will* be there to sustain you and protect you. If He has called you to something, He will give you the strength you need to accomplish it.

I Am Not Ashamed

Rejoicing Freely When God Moves

By Jennette Rogers, Anderson University

However, if you suffer as a Christian, do not be ashamed,
but praise God that you bear that name.

1 PETER 4:16

I was completely embarrassed. Did my friend not see me squirming in my seat? I thought she'd pick up the hints I was sending her way. But, of course, she didn't.

It was the summer between my sophomore and junior years of high school. My best friend, Nicole, and I had been out shopping at the mall. As usual, we made a stop at the local 31 Flavors ice-cream shop. We were enjoying pecan praline and mint chocolate chip, and Nicole was telling me about some amazing things happening in her church. They were having a revival, and God was moving in the hearts of unbelievers. Nicole was usually a very loud person, but that day she was more boisterous than usual—or at least I thought so.

She kept talking, but the only point I could concentrate on was how loud she was and how the other people in the ice-cream shop could hear every word she said. I became embarrassed for her—or rather *of* her. I kept trying to get her to speak more softly by responding in a very muted tone, but she didn't seem to notice.

It was not until a couple of weeks later, when another friend and I were at a Christian concert, that I realized what I had been feeling that day. The concert featured a number of Christian musicians. One in particular stood out to me—or at least her message did. "I am not ashamed," she kept singing clearly and purely. "I am not ashamed to bear Your name."

As she sang, I realized that in the ice-cream shop, I had been ashamed of letting others know I was a Christian. I had been embarrassed by Nicole's excitement for the new believers in her church. Instead of rejoicing publicly with my friend, I had been trying to hush her joy to save myself from embarrassment.

As the song continued, I sang along—with a loud voice—shouting out to God that I was no longer ashamed of Him.

I left the concert wanting to share my faith more than ever before. I realized that instead of trying to hush my friend, I should have been trying to minister to those other ice-cream lovers. I understood that to be a true minister of God, I must not be ashamed to rejoice when others find salvation.

Wisdom for the Week

DAY 1: ROMANS 1:13-17;
          1 CORINTHIANS 2:1-5
DAY 2: COLOSSIANS 2:1-7
DAY 3: GALATIANS 1:13-17
DAY 4: ACTS 2:22-27
DAY 5: 1 CORINTHIANS 2:1-5

Speaking Up

Talking to people about God isn't always easy. Here are a few considerations that might make sharing your faith just a little less daunting:

- **You're not selling anything**. All you need to do is tell your story and maybe answer some questions. You're just telling someone about something good that happened to you. That doesn't sound so hard, does it? "God did not give us a spirit of timidity, but a spirit of power, of love and of self-discipline. So do not be ashamed to testify about our Lord" (2 Timothy 1:7-8).

- **You don't need to know everything.** Sure, there are tough theological questions out there—but what are the chances anyone's going to ask you one of them? Stick to what you *do* understand—your love for Jesus—and be willing to admit what you don't know. This isn't a debate; it's just a conversation. "For it is God who works in you to will and to act according to his good purpose" (Philippians 2:13).

- **You're not a telemarketer**. Evangelism isn't a script you rattle off every time someone makes eye contact with you. You don't have to be rude or forceful—just try not to waste any opportunities God sends your way. "So then, just as you received Christ Jesus as Lord, continue to live in him, rooted and built up in him, strengthened in the faith as you were taught, and overflowing with thankfulness" (Colossians 2:6).

9

Come What May

Waiting on God Through the Pain

By Ryan Smernoff, Biola University

So do not fear, for I am with you; do not be dismayed,
for I am your God. I will strengthen you and help you; I will
uphold you with my righteous right hand.

ISAIAH 41:10

My community-college career began with my father being diagnosed with cancer, and it ended with my father dying from that cancer. Through that time, I found myself doing whatever I could to stay away from home to avoid the heartbreak of watching my father waste away. But no matter how much I tried to dodge the situation, nothing was going to stop my father from dying, not even God.

What made matters even worse was that I knew that my father's death would make it financially impossible for me to transfer to the private university to which I had been accepted. I found myself spending much of my days doing two things: searching for scholarships and praying that God would somehow provide the money I needed to get an education. After about a year of this daily ritual, I nearly gave up on prayer.

This isn't one of those stories where God miraculously heals someone—my father died, and I was devastated.

Then one day about six weeks after my father's death, God did something I never expected. I came home and heard my mother crying as I walked through the front door. After what we had been through, this wasn't surprising, but today her cry sounded different. Her sniffles were punctuated with small bursts of laughter, and her tears were diverted by a large smile. I wanted to know what had happened, but before I could ask, my mother blurted it out: "Someone has offered to pay your way through college!"

Apparently, a generous and anonymous individual had learned of my predicament and wanted to cover all of the costs of my college tuition, housing and books. God had decided to answer my prayers, and He did so in a way that left no doubt that He really is in control of all things.

In times of tragedy, it's easy to lose trust in God. How can we honestly believe that God has a perfect plan when we see so much pain around us? The only answer is simply to wait on God. Whether we know it or not, God works with a purpose—one that we should never wish to divert, no matter what the cost.

Wisdom for the Week

DAY 1: ISAIAH 44:6-8

DAY 2: PSALM 33:12-22

DAY 3: PSALM 119:25-32

DAY 4: PROVERBS 19:17-21

DAY 5: ROMANS 8:1-5;
        1 CHRONICLES 29:10-19

What Kind of Computer Do I Need for School?

Before you go out and purchase a new computer for school, you might want to keep the following points in mind:

- Desktops are okay, but laptops are more portable.

- Check with the school before buying a computer to see if the campus store offers student purchase or rental discounts on computer equipment.

- Make sure the computer is equipped with all the necessary hardware and software, especially for wireless Internet capability and up-to-date virus protection programs.

- If you get a laptop, invest in a sturdy carrying case.

- Consider getting insurance for lost, stolen or damaged computer equipment.

- Do not leave computers unattended in student lounge areas, cafeterias, libraries or bookstore cubbies—no matter how safe they may seem.

10

Stick with It

Persevering When the Going Gets Tough

By Jeff Hill, Biola University

But if we hope for what we do not see, with
perseverance we wait eagerly for it.
ROMANS 8:25, *NASB*

It was a scorching Friday afternoon in Southern California, and I had just driven 20 hours to begin my sophomore year as a transfer student. I pulled up to the curb outside my new residence hall and started unloading the goods: clothes, computer, deodorant, pillow—all the things college students take to school. I won't say I was nervous; I just didn't know what to expect. I had never lived so far from home.

During the summer, I'd gotten my housing information and found out I would be sharing a room with my new university's student-body president. Me? A transfer-nobody living with the president of the school? This was thrilling news, but I knew it would be tough for me—the new guy rooming with the coolest kid on campus.

Our first meeting was awkward. We exchanged a few timid words and began putting our stuff away in separate corners of the room. The sun was slowly falling, and I was getting ready for my first night's sleep in my new home. When I was done unpacking, I quietly climbed to the top of the bunks. My new roommate stood below looking up at me. "This semester I want to serve you," he told me unexpectedly. "Please be yourself."

Those encouraging words were just what I needed. I had been wondering for some time why I was making this jaunt so far south. It had been a daunting decision. But after hearing my new roommate's words, I told myself I was going to give this place some time. I'd stick with my decision to come to this campus, and I'd make the most of it. I'm thankful I did.

With those simple words from my new roommate that first night and his continued encouragement in the months to come, I became involved with just about every activity on campus. Eventually I even became Orientation Director, which gives me the opportunity to assist new students with *their* transition to a new school life. I often find myself telling the weary, broken, unsure and unconvinced student, "You may not be sure right now, but stick with it. I think you'll end up loving it."

Now it's my last semester of college and I'm applying to graduate schools, where I will again start over in a new place. I thank God that He led me to a school that I fell in love with, and I'm thankful that my roommate's encouragement helped me stick through a bewildering transition.

Wisdom for the Week

DAY 1: PSALM 3:3-8

DAY 2: PROVERBS 15:13-33

DAY 3: PSALMS 92:1-9; 57:7-11

DAY 4: 2 CORINTHIANS 1:5-11

DAY 5: PROVERBS 12:25-28

What to Pack for College

School Supplies
- Notebooks and paper
- Pens and pencils
- Scissors
- Calculator
- File folders
- Calendar, daily planner or PDA
- Dictionary and thesaurus

Personal Items
- Grooming supplies
- Shower caddy
- Flip-flops
- Bible
- Pictures from home
- Sports equipment (Frisbee, baseball, bat, glove, football, etc.)

Linens
- Towels and washcloths
- Sheets and pillowcases
- Blanket and/or comforter
- Laundry bag or basket, and detergent

Electronics
- Computer
- Extension cord and/or power strip
- Alarm clock
- Phone or phone cards
- Camera
- Desk lamp

Items Roommates Might Share
- Iron
- Stereo
- Television
- DVD player
- Printer (and ink cartridges)
- Coffeemaker
- Microwave
- Compact refrigerator
- Bulletin board
- Trash container (and trash bags)
- Hammer and screwdriver

11

Letting Go of Pride

Learning Humility Through Homesickness

By Hannah Bishop, Biola University

For by the grace given me I say to every one of you:
Do not think of yourself more highly than you ought, but rather
think of yourself with sober judgment, in accordance with
the measure of faith God has given you.

ROMANS 12:3

I can't even begin to explain how thrilled I was to be leaving my small hometown in Washington for a university in Southern California. I was finally leaving the moldy old town I had grown up in and all the poor saps who hung around there. I felt superior to my friends who didn't leave home after high school—as if I was better than them because I could forget about my life and leave it all behind.

It didn't take long for my smugness to trip me up. Two weeks into the semester, homesickness slapped me in the face. I cried every night. I was lonely and miserable and completely overwhelmed. Every time my parents called, I begged them to buy me a plane ticket home.

It finally sunk in that I was no better than the kids I left behind in my Washington hometown. I was weak, vulnerable and incapable of handling all the stress I felt. Change scared me. I felt thousands of miles from home.

God humbled me in those difficult weeks by using my homesickness to expose my arrogance. Sure, it had been brave of me to leave home and pursue my education—but could I really claim to be better than all those people I knew who got jobs delivering pizza or who were taking a class or two at the local JC?

As I began to acknowledge my conceit, I looked for ways to root it out of myself: I talked to people at home more often and tried not to stereotype them as lazy or brainless because they weren't attending a university. I also thought twice before I judged another's decision about work or college. Many individuals weren't as fortunate as I—a lot of them had financial concerns, family conflicts and other problems I didn't have to struggle with. I learned to understand those difficulties and appreciate all that I have.

Sure, my homesickness was difficult, but God used it to reveal my judgmental character. Learn from my mistakes. Avoid criticizing others based on their decisions; you don't know what it's like to live in their skin. Just be thankful for what you have and love others unconditionally.

Wisdom for the Week

DAY 1: PROVERBS 13:10-16

DAY 2: PSALM 10:1-4

DAY 3: PROVERBS 16:16-19

DAY 4: PSALM 20:6-9

DAY 5: 1 CORINTHIANS 3:18-23

Top Campus Jobs Held by Undergraduate Students

1. Teaching assistant

2. Science-laboratory stockroom clerk

3. Library assistant

4. Campus dining-hall service worker

5. University bookstore clerk

6. College admissions office intern

7. Financial-aid department office assistant

8. Technical and media support person

9. Campus safety officer

10. Learning center/writing center tutor or consultant

God Moments

Blessing When You Least Expect It

By Emily E. Bennett, Biola University

Your love, O LORD, reaches to the heavens, your faithfulness to the skies. Your righteousness is like the mighty mountains, your justice like the great deep.

PSALM 36:5-6

I spent the first three weeks of college trudging around campus, overwhelmed and bogged down—literally. I was a 110-pound science major with a load of books almost half my weight. With back-to-back classes, my clumsy freshman hands were constantly occupied with lugging around a stack of books. Every day I managed to drop them while opening doors or maneuvering through crowded hallways. In the big courtyard with the fountain where everyone hangs out, I inevitably lost my balance and stumbled. My books scattered, and my face turned 10 shades darker than my red hair.

In addition to book problems, I dealt with other issues. I felt unloved, alone and disconnected. I doubted anyone was even aware of my existence. I had just become another student number among thousands of others. My days were consumed with study, and between academics and work, I had no time to connect with anybody.

One night as I plodded up the gloomy stairwell, another nursing student approached me. Excitedly she asked if I wanted to see what she had bought that day. Tired, I reluctantly plodded along beside her as she opened her shopping bag. She pulled out some jeans and then a nifty black book bag. Like a true science major, she explained in detail the purpose of each gadget and pocket on the bag. She handed it over for me to inspect. She smiled. "Do you like it?" she asked.

"Yeah!" I told her. "It's great."

"Well," she said, "it's for you!"

I was genuinely stunned by her kindness. She told me that when she saw the bag, she thought of me and my desperate book battles. For the first time since I had moved, I felt like somebody was aware of my existence and actually cared. My heart was warmed by her loving gesture. How wonderful to feel God respond to my longings through another person!

This is what I like to call a God Moment—a random point in the midst of a busy life when God makes Himself known. A God Moment is a small yet obvious blessing that sometimes remains unnoticed but makes life worth living, when God works through other people to show His love.

As you make your way through this busy day, keep your eyes open for the little ways God will make Himself known to you—and ways you can make Him known to others. God Moments happen all the time. We have only to stop and notice them.

Wisdom for the Week

DAY 1: ROMANS 8:38-39

DAY 2: LUKE 6:15-21

DAY 3: MALACHI 3:10-12

DAY 4: 2 KINGS 4:1-7

DAY 5: 2 CORINTHIANS 8:1-4

Random Acts of Kindness

Do a kind act "for goodness sake." Has a friend's unexpected compliment or a stranger's generosity ever just made your day? Take a moment this week to do the same for someone else.

- Pay a friend an honest compliment.

- Put a quarter in a stranger's expired parking meter.

- Give a cookie, some candy or a flower (don't filch from campus landscapes!) to a cashier, cafeteria worker or someone else who works at your college.

- Write a note of appreciation to someone who has helped, encouraged or inspired you.

- Buy your professor a cup of coffee or a soft drink.

- Open a door for someone.

- Join someone who's eating alone in the cafeteria.

- Pick up litter on your way to class.

- Visit or send a note to a person who is sick or shut-in.

Making the Effort

Living in Peace with Roommates

By Angela Story, Southeastern University

Make every effort to live at peace with all.
HEBREWS 12: 14

Plain walls, empty desks, bare floors—dorm rooms often leave much to be desired. As two eager freshmen, my roommate and I met the day we moved in. We found instant friendship, and right away we agreed that our room needed spice. After a trip to Wal-Mart that yielded colorful posters, vibrant rugs, scented candles and cheerful curtains, the room looked and felt just the way I liked it: cozy, comfortable and very clean.

However, to my dismay, the small homey space quickly became a monstrous disaster area. Piles of clothes lay heaped in every corner. Stacks of books, folders and loose sheets of paper spilled across the floor. Food wrappers, soda cans and half-empty water bottles littered the whole area. Clearly my roommate did not value housekeeping the way I did.

One day, frantic because I couldn't find a notebook under her layers of junk, I exploded in a scathing tirade that left her in tears. I instantly felt guilty about my outburst, but at the same time, my roommate's messy habits aggravated me. Sharing a living space had proved to be much more difficult than I'd anticipated. With three and a half months left in the semester,

I knew that we needed a peaceful resolution—fast.

During my devotion later that day, the Lord spoke to me and I realized that I was part of the problem. Not wanting to anger my new friend, I had given no indication that her slovenly habits bothered me in the least. My silence had resulted in a building, blistering rage that threatened not only the peace in our room but also our friendship.

That night, we had a calm heart-to-heart, and we can both testify that simple communication works wonders. Of course, our room did not suddenly become the immaculate haven I envisioned at the beginning of the year, and I'm sure she could catalogue times when I annoyed her. Nevertheless, the experience taught us about compromise and love, and we are fortunate to remain friends to this day.

Living with a roommate is a definite challenge; sooner or later conflicts will arise. When they do, it's up to us to do everything we can to live at peace with each other. Our God can work through any situation when we obey His Word.

Wisdom for the Week

DAY 1: PSALM 119:9-16
DAY 2: MATTHEW 5:1-12
DAY 3: ROMANS 14:13-19
DAY 4: PSALM 31:1-5
DAY 5: PROVERBS 17:1-14

Bargain Sources for Dorm Decorating

- Thrift stores (Salvation Army, Goodwill)

- Local consignment shops

- Bargain stores (Big Lots, Dollar Store, Dollar Tree)

- Big discount stores (Wal-Mart, Kmart, Target)

- Small discount retailers and outlet stores (TJ Maxx, Marshalls, Ross)

- Import stores (Pier One, Cost Plus World Market, Ikea)

- Home-improvement stores (Lowe's, Home Depot, Menards)

- Houseware stores (Linens 'n Things; Bed, Bath and Beyond)

- Online auction and discount Internet sites

- Last but not least, scavenge items from friends and family

14

Growth in Wisdom, Increase in Sorrow

Through Uncertainty to Understanding

By Candice Hansard, Biola University

For with much wisdom comes much sorrow;
the more knowledge, the more grief.
ECCLESIASTES 1:18

The first semester of my freshman year was only minutes from beginning. I was thrilled. The next chapter of my life was about to start, and I could hardly wait. When I woke up for my first day of classes, I was eager to learn and grow in every possible way. I went to my first course and was amazed at how big the room was. Surrounded by 200 other students, I listened to the professor lecture, realizing I was officially a college student. My professor was a genius. Every word that came from his mouth was so rich and sweet that I couldn't help but revel in the wisdom he shared with me.

As the weeks passed, I still loved going to class, but I faced a challenge I hadn't expected. As I began to grow intellectually, I realized how little I really knew. At first this insight spurred me to learn more, but I soon grew discouraged by the vast amounts of untouched material out there for me to grasp. By the end of the semester, the biggest lesson I had learned was that I knew practically nothing. On top of that, no one else seemed to agree with the few things I thought I did know—so my life filled not only with impossible questions but with exhausting strife as well. I felt at war with myself, questioning everything I thought I knew. Nothing was easy. There were no longer yes and no answers. Learning wasn't simple anymore. Was obtaining new wisdom worth all the pain I was feeling?

As I look back on my first semester as a college intellectual, I see that wisdom is, indeed, worth the struggle, and I (in my best moments) enjoy wrestling with the issues before me. The struggle can be discouraging, and it causes much sorrow and uncertainty, but in the long run, it will be good for me. From this strife, will come a true understanding of who I am and what I believe.

Wisdom for the Week

DAY 1: DEUTERONOMY 4:5-7
DAY 2: 1 KINGS 4:28-30
DAY 3: PROVERBS 4:6-8
DAY 4: ECCLESIASTES 7:10-12
DAY 5: JEREMIAH 7:22-24

How to Get Your Professors to Like You

Do . . .

- Introduce yourself the first day of class (give a firm handshake, make eye contact and smile).
- Talk to him or her (at least pretend they're human beings!). Laugh at their jokes.
- Sit toward the front of the classroom.
- Participate in class discussions. Ask good questions when no one else will talk.
- Show interest in the course content. Take notes.
- Turn in assignments on time.
- Ask for help when you need it.
- Drop by their offices or classrooms just to say hello.
- Bake them cookies.
- Be sincere. Be polite (say "Thank you" and mean it). Be funny. Be smart. Be honest.
- Turn off your cell phone before class.

Don't . . .

- Come to class late.
- Cheat.
- Act rudely or resentfully.
- Sleep in class.
- Ask ridiculous or irrelevant questions.
- Talk while professors are talking.
- Take cell phone calls in class.
- Slouch in the back row and stare out the window.
- Assume the worst about your instructors.

15

Let Them Eat Steak

Sharing with Enemies Can Make Them Friends

By William Crawford, Biola University

If your enemy is hungry, give him food to eat; if he is thirsty, give him water to drink.

PROVERBS 25:21

Don't you love those proverbs that don't seem to apply to you? The ones that command absurd actions in bizarre situations you will never find yourself in? Me, too. I wish the Bible had some of those.

When I came to college, I brought along a knack for cooking that I'd picked up in high school. It's a very useful skill that few guys have a firm grasp on. (Guys, listen: Learn to cook, if only because girls love it!) This ability made me popular with the other guys in the dorm—my reputation spread, and if someone wanted a quick lesson in the culinary arts or a good home-cooked meal, he came to me.

However, there was one guy in the dorm—whom I will call Micah—who stood out. While others enjoyed the cinnamon rolls and pies I baked, Micah seemed to resent my cooking skills and the attention it gave me. We couldn't even carry on a decent conversation without Micah getting sarcastic. His tone was always spiteful and his words angry. "Oh, you're so awesome," he might say derisively, "just because you *cook*!" I put up with his jealous sarcasm for weeks.

One night I cooked a steak dinner for some friends, and Micah sauntered into the dorm kitchen where we were eating. He'd missed dinner, and he was starved. Resisting my natural impulse to enjoy tormenting him by eating in front of him, I offered him a cut of steak and a biscuit. He gladly took the plate I offered and chowed down.

While eating, it seemed to dawn on Micah that it was *my* food he was eating—*me*, the guy whom he had gone out of his way to mock! (And it was darn good food, if I do say so myself.) Micah thanked me several times on the spot. And just like that, everything changed between us. From that point on, we had a friendship of sorts. His attitude changed about me, as did mine about him. No jealousy. No insults. We were suddenly on the same side—and we have been ever since. All it took was some steak and a biscuit.

This is the truth Proverbs 25:21 speaks. In the utterly uncanny instance when I had a choice to feed my enemy or let him go hungry, I swallowed my pride and followed the wisdom of God's Word. He blessed Micah and me with friendship because of it.

Let my story encourage you to examine your own repertoire of skills and share them with someone who needs them, even if that person does not like you . . . yet. After all, the book of Proverbs sometimes sounds crazy, but it is never wrong.

Wisdom for the Week

DAY 1: 1 SAMUEL 26:18-25

DAY 2: LUKE 6:27-36

DAY 3: MATTHEW 6:9-15

DAY 4: LUKE 6:27-36

DAY 5: 1 JOHN 2:4-12

Ten Favorite Dorm-Room Foods

1. Popcorn

2. Crackers (especially Goldfish)

3. Macaroni and cheese

4. Instant noodles (such as ramen)

5. Cereal and oatmeal

6. Chocolate

7. Peanut butter and jelly

8. Chips and salsa

9. Bagels

10. Yogurt

16

Loaning My Sandals to Jesus

Loving My Roommate as I Love Christ

By Katleyn Pollet, Montreat College

Love your neighbor as yourself.

MATTHEW 22:39

When I was growing up, my sister and I avoided sharing our toys if we could. Our mentality was, "This is mine, so you can't play with it." When I moved into college my freshman year, the change was drastic. Adjusting was hard.

It was near the beginning of the year, and I had known my roommate for only two months. One sunny day, I was in the cafeteria eating lunch. My day was going great until my roommate walked through the cafeteria doors. She was wearing my flip-flops, shirt, earrings and necklace. Usually it was not a big deal to me if she borrowed my clothes, but today was different! Some of the things she wore were brand-new, which I'm sure had something to do with my reaction. Whatever the reason, I was really ticked off.

I faced a crossroads in our relationship. I had two directions to choose from: I could do what came naturally and walk over to angrily tell her how I felt about her wearing my clothes, or I could cling to the Lord's strength and *love her as I love myself*. Sitting in the cafeteria that day, I chose to seek the Lord's path—but it was not easy. I was able to swallow my pride and wait till later to talk to her in the dorm. When the time was right, I told her what was on my heart and how I truly felt. I also explained how I was raised so that she could understand why I was so bothered.

She had no idea that what she did might be seen as rude. She had grown up much different from me. In her house, everyone shared everything. She did not claim what was hers as *hers*. She assumed, because we lived together, that we would share everything.

After that day, it was a struggle to constantly put my room-mate before me, but I came to realize how much more impor-tant it is to love people than to let material things get in the way. I also learned how to love people through sharing what I have. I know that if Jesus wanted to wear my sandals, I would let Him without thinking twice. I would give Him everything I owned if He asked for it. God has slowly been teaching me that I should love other people the same way.

We are called to love and serve others the same way we love and serve Christ—the same way He loves and serves us. God used my roommate to humble me and to give me a glimpse of what it looks like to die to myself and to live for Christ.

Wisdom for the Week

DAY 1: PROVERBS 25:9-15

DAY 2: LEVITICUS 19:13-18

DAY 3: 2 CORINTHIANS 12:8-10

DAY 4: 1 PETER 4: 8-14

DAY 5: JOHN 14:10-15

Conflict

When two people live in close proximity, conflict *will* happen. When your roommate snaps at you for rearranging his graphic novel collection or when she cranks up her Dixie Chicks album for the fifth time that day, here are a few things to remember:

- **What you're arguing about might be a symptom.** We all come to college with different histories and notions of what's acceptable and where our boundaries are. Backing up a few steps from the present squabble and talking about our roots can prevent a lot of future conflicts.

- **Count on it: You drive your roommate crazy, too.** Something you do probably makes your roommate want to scream. So when you complain to your roommate about his knuckle cracking or her overflowing laundry hamper, be willing to let the conversation turn to your own foibles and idiosyncrasies.

- **Look for a win-win solution.** It's usually healthier to negotiate than argue. In an argument, each person is trying to make the other lose. In a negotiation, each person is trying to find a solution in the best interest of both parties.

- **Conflict isn't necessarily bad.** Roommates are like two rocks in a sack—they grind a lot at first, but over time they smooth out each other's rough edges and polish each other's personalities. All this friction might actually be good for you in the long run.

The Bells Toll

Following God's Song

By Ryan Horner, Point Loma Nazarene University

Deep calls to deep in the roar of your waterfalls;
all your waves and breakers have swept over me.

PSALM 42:7

I spent this past fall studying in London. One cool October evening, I took a walk in a park amidst the bustle of the city. It was autumn, and a carpet of leaves crunched beneath the weight of my feet. The night seemed gloomier than usual and tinged with a sense of sadness that instilled in me a mood of somber contemplation.

Then, suddenly, the air was filled with the indescribable song of church bells. I lifted my head and looked around me. I wasn't sure why, but I felt as if I heard God's whisper, telling me that I should follow the sound of the bells. Reluctantly I submitted and let my footsteps follow the sounds.

I finally came upon an old gothic church. The streets all around were empty, but the clanging bells filled the night. I walked through a dark graveyard beyond the church building and sat on a bench amidst a dilapidated garden of stone. As I brooded in the darkness, a pale blue and purple light danced on my clothes—light from a sky that was clouded over but still had a touch of brightness in it.

I eventually went inside the church and found that only four or five other people had come to the service. We quietly sang a few hymns. We prayed together for our troubled world. We listened to the pastor's brief message—nothing particularly inspiring or out of the ordinary. And then it dawned on me: For one of the few times in my life, I felt as if I was exactly where God wanted me.

I had submitted to a whisper that often gets drowned out by my will, my fears, my selfishness and the noise and bustle of my busy life. I was ready to go my own way, as I almost always am, but instead I let something become real that was higher, deeper and brighter than any thought my imagination could conjure. It didn't involve momentous floods of emotion, just soft and subtle ripples of well-being that reminded me I could let it all go and be safe as I fell into loving arms.

> *As he that sees a dark and shady grove,*
> *Stays not, but looks beyond it on the sky*
> *So when I view my sins, mine eyes remove*
> *More backward still, and to that water fly,*
> *Which is above the heav'ns, whose spring and rent*
> *Is in my dear Redeemer's pierced side.*
> GEORGE HERBERT, "HOLY BAPTISM (I)"

Wisdom for the Week

DAY 1: PSALM 71:1-8

DAY 2: MATTHEW 9:18-22

DAY 3: ACTS 9:22-31

DAY 4: ISAIAH 40:1-5

DAY 5: JOHN 14:16-20

And Don't Forget Your Toothbrush

Many universities offer economical study-abroad semesters. These programs can be great opportunities, but there's bound to be some homesickness. Here are some things to keep in mind before you catch your flight to help you have a happy, well-adjusted semester far from home:

- **Keep in touch with people back home.** Email or find space on the Internet where you can post updates and pictures (www.myspace.com is a good place to get a free account). Long-distance phone calls can be expensive, but Skype (www.skype.com) is a terrific (and cheap!) instant-messaging service. Provided you both have speakers and microphones, you can talk free of charge to people anywhere in the world.

- **Try to imagine what you'll miss.** Part of the fun of traveling is trying new cuisine, but every once in a while you'll want a meal like the ones back home. Bring favorite family recipes or other familiar items you know you'll miss, like favorite toiletries or snack bars. Just try not to use them all the first week!

- **Form a support group with fellow travelers.** It helps immensely to be among other friendly foreigners who are making the same mistakes and learning the same ropes.

- **Find a church.** Being rooted in a community of fellowship is another way to feel more at home and settled when you are studying overseas.

—Kathy Zazzara, Biola University

18

The Deepest Parts

Welcoming Grief to the Table

By Hillary Prag, Seattle Pacific University

Let them lie face down in the dust; then at last there is hope for them.
LAMENTATIONS 3:29, NLT

Grief is the black ox that I lead around with me wherever I go these days. It is a huge, distracting beast of burden that takes up a great deal of space and attention. It has been lumbering awkwardly beside me since I began this process of grieving and will continue to be here, stepping on my feet and crowding me until I am finished. Then I'll send it to market and everyone who has been cheering for me in this process will celebrate with great ceremony. In the meantime, I am learning to make room in my life for something that's messy and heavy.

I have never been more exhausted than when I was told to look grief straight in the face and step aside as it walked into my living room. I lay on the floor and sobbed until I was dizzy. I had to decide to trust that God was big enough to bear this burden with me. Some days I cannot carry my share of the burden, and the very thought of it makes me shaky. These are the times when I picture God slapping His forehead and rolling His eyes because the entire point is for me to realize that I need not bear any burden on my own. God is in the business of running out to meet me in my place of despair.

Our Christian culture sometimes teaches us that when God shows up in our moment of grief, He will relieve our pain immediately upon arrival. We panic if Lazarus looks like he's taken another turn for the worse. Yet Jesus didn't show up until after Mary and Martha had been suffering for four days. He seemed to see the importance of their grief—sorrow gave them so much more joy in the end. Jesus allowed the process to occur in His own life, too. He made space in His last few hours on Earth for moments of despair that turned His sweat to blood. He welcomed the cup of suffering rather than shying away from it.

We, on the other hand, are adept at ushering grief out of our lives. We don't know much about welcoming it to the table. Trust that you do not have to welcome it alone. God will show you how to dance with your black ox, a guest that will leave you richer and stronger. But first you must be willing to open the door and stand aside.

I am pretty sure that it is only by experiencing that ocean of sadness in a naked and immediate way that we come to be healed— which is to say that we come to experience life with a real sense of presence and spaciousness and peace.

ANNE LAMOTT

Wisdom for the Week

DAY 1: JOB 5:6-11
DAY 2: PSALM 18:1-6; JOHN 11:17-25
DAY 3: 2 SAMUEL 22:1-7; 1 JOHN 5:13-15
DAY 4: PSALM 3:1-8; 2 CORINTHIANS 7:4-8
DAY 5: 2 CHRONICLES 14:8-13

When Someone You Know Is Grieving

Grief is something most of us will eventually go through. Even if you've been blessed never to experience it yourself, chances are that someone you know will. Here are some things to keep in mind if someone you know is grieving:

- **Don't avoid the person.** When a person is grieving, the situation is often made worse by feelings of abandonment. After all, who isn't going to feel awkward knocking on the door of a person down the hall who has recently lost a loved one? You don't have to pry, but don't avoid the person and don't avoid the subject.

- **Listen.** If your friend wants to talk, don't panic. All you have to do is listen. You don't need to come up with brilliant advice or wrack your brain for some experience you've had that will show your friend that you know what he or she is going through. Most of the time, your friend will just want someone to listen.

- **You don't need to cheer the person up.** Cheering your friend up isn't really the goal. Grief is a real and very difficult process. Let your friend go through it in his or her own way. Walk beside your friend as he or she goes through the process, and your friend will always remember what you did when he or she comes out the other side.

- **Pray.** Maybe your friend doesn't feel comfortable enough for you to pray *with* him or her, but you can always pray *for* that person. Do it any time you think of your friend.

19

With Friends Like These

Partying Away the Good Life

By John David, Azusa Pacific University

Who has woe? Who has sorrow? Who has strife? Who has complaints? Who has needless bruises? Who has bloodshot eyes? Those who linger over wine, who go to sample bowls of mixed wine. Do not gaze at wine when it is red, when it sparkles in the cup, when it flows down smoothly! In the end it bites like a snake and poisons like a viper.

PROVERBS 23:29-32

College and drinking—the two sometimes seem to go hand in hand. When I got to college, the first thing I did was look for the party. It was the most familiar thing to me—I was a football player from a public high school—and it seemed the easiest way to meet people at my new school.

I figured college was about experimentation and growth, but I soon fell into the trap of partying way too much. My grades didn't suffer, but my good godly friendships did, as well as my relationship with the Lord. I became more bitter and less Christlike. I was living that double life our Sunday School teachers warned us about.

I remember one specific weekend: It was Halloween and my birthday was the next day. My friends and I were at a house famous for its parties, and some of my buddies gave me a bottle of rum for a birthday present. By the end of the night, the bottle was empty and I had passed out in the truck bed of my friend's pickup, which was in a parking lot.

It rained that night.

When my friends found me soaked to the bone, they just left me in the back of the pickup and drove home. They helped me to my dorm room and put me in my bed—but not before they wrote all over my body with a magic marker. My drinking amused them. When I went home for my birthday the next day, completely hungover, I had to pretend I was sick.

Take it from someone who has been there: Alcohol—like a lot of things you might associate with college—can be a snare, and it's a good idea to avoid it.

Not long after that wild weekend, I woke up one morning and felt a huge hole in my life. I realized that college *is* about growing and exploring new things—hand in hand with God and with good solid friends, rather than with friends who find pleasure and amusement in your life's downward spiral. College is about learning your limitations and learning to avoid the traps you're most likely to fall into.

Wisdom for the Week

DAY 1: 1 CORINTHIANS 15:33-34

DAY 2: PROVERBS 31:4-9

DAY 3: LUKE 21:29-36

DAY 4: PROVERBS 1:10-19

DAY 5: GALATIANS 5:16-24

Nail-Biting Nomenclature

In honor of Halloween, a traditionally scary day, here are some phobias you might want to check yourself for:

- *Coulrophobia*—fear of clowns
- *Dromophobia*—fear of crossing streets
- *Lachanophobia*—fear of vegetables
- *Carnophobia*—fear of meat
- *Pediophobia*—fear of dolls
- *Aulophobia*—fear of flutes
- *Pentheraphobia*—fear of mother-in-law
- *Barophobia*—fear of gravity
- *Melissophobia*—fear of bees
- *Homichlophobia*—fear of fog
- *Nephophobia*—fear of clouds
- *Peladophobia*—fear of bald people
- *Phalacrophobia*—fear of becoming bald
- *Pogonophobia*—fear of beards
- *Dextrophobia*—fear of objects on the right
- *Sinistrophobia*—fear of objects on the left
- *Logizomechanophobia*—fear of computers
- *Metrophobia*—fear of poetry
- *Ephebiphobia*—fear of teenagers
- *Glossophobia*—fear of speaking in public
- *Hippopotomonstrosesquippedaliophobia*—fear of long words
- *Triskaidekaphobia*—fear of the number 13
- *Paraskavedekatriaphobia*—fear of Friday the 13th
- *Samhainophobia*—fear of Halloween

—Heather Buchanan, Chapman University

20

Unequally Yoked?

Honestly Addressing Interfaith Relationships

By Keena Betta, Wellesley College

Do not be yoked together with unbelievers.
For what do righteousness and wickedness have in common?
Or what fellowship can light have with darkness?
2 CORINTHIANS 6:14

If you've been around the Church awhile, you've probably given or received advice about dating. Terms like "courtship" and "DTR" are thrown around, but many of us still have difficulty navigating our dating lives. There's a third term that frequently comes up, and it's one that I've grappled with in the past several years: "unequally yoked." I didn't always understand God's good design for Christian marriage. In fact, I've been involved in romantic relationships with non-Christian men—despite my seeking after Christ for many years.

I once dated a man whose motto for our relationship was "More church, more baseball"—meaning that he hoped attending church with me would lead to sexual favors for him. Obviously, such a viewpoint was incompatible with my beliefs, and it put undue stress on our relationship. And the stress wasn't all his doing: I placed a ridiculous amount of pressure on him to explore religious issues.

Imagine if I'd followed through to marriage—would that man have understood my decision to tithe? Would he have supported my desire to attend seminary? Would he have allowed me to bring our children up in the Church? Faith was a huge part of my life, and a man who didn't share my faith could never really share my life. The truth is, I didn't trust Christ to provide for my needs and desires.

As students, we need to be prepared for connections with people outside our Christian experience—this is a critical part of college and also of our ministry as Christ's representative on our campus. But we should also be aware of unhealthy attachments to non-Christians. If we've spent most of our growing up years in Christian community, it can come as a surprise that non-Christians are not all horrible—many are generous, kind and commitment-minded people—and we can be unwillingly attracted to them, despite our intentions.

Yet such attractions have the power to derail our walk, so be wary. Are you spending too much time with an unbelieving member of the opposite sex? Are you denying the reality of a romantic connection by saying the relationship is part of your "evangelism" efforts? Be honest about these interfaith relationships so that an emotional connection does not catch you unaware.

Remember: Your ultimate hope is in Christ, no matter how far you've strayed or what situations you're facing. Christ can empower and guide you to make God-centered choices in your romantic life.

*A woman's heart should be so close to the Lord
that a man has to seek after Him just to find her.*

Wisdom for the Week

DAY 1: GENESIS 2:18-24

DAY 2: PHILIPPIANS 3:7-10

DAY 3: 1 CORINTHIANS 5:9-11

DAY 4: PSALM 25:14-22

DAY 5: PSALM 31:21-24

Dating Guidelines?

Some dating experiences are more hilarious than meaningful. Here are some lighthearted guidelines for avoiding the disaster date:

How to Know When He's Not the Right Guy for You

- *Every* night is a Blockbuster night.
- He winks at your mom when he comes to pick you up.
- He takes longer to get ready than you do.
- He's got a probation officer.
- He thinks barbeque sauce is a side dish.

How to Know When She's Not the Right Girl for You

- She orders the most expensive items on the menu on the first date.
- She's always offering to pluck your eyebrows.
- She talks to you in a baby voice.
- By your second date, she's already scrapbooked your first date.
- You met her on MySpace.

21

When the Heart Is Ready

Trusting that God Is at Work in a Friend's Life

By Jennifer Hare, University of California, San Diego

But you must return to your God; maintain love and justice,
and wait for your God always.

HOSEA 12:6

I first met Shane when we both showed up at the wrong time and the wrong place for the first day of grammar class. From then on, we kept crossing paths in spontaneous and unexpected ways until I began to wonder, *Did God bring us together for a reason?* I decided to invite him to an InterVarsity fellowship event one night on campus. The topic was "A Case for the Resurrection: Did Jesus Really Rise from the Dead?" I'd heard it was a good opportunity to invite seekers and nonbelievers into the Christian community in a way that wasn't intimidating.

But when the message began, *I* was the intimidated one! The whole time, I was worried that Shane was bored or confused or that the guest speaker was too defensive, too aggressive, too preachy. I wasn't even able to enjoy the worship music afterward because I was afraid Shane might think it was lame. I honestly wanted God to change Shane's life, but I had made up my mind that tonight was not the night.

Then someone came up to the front of the room and said, "Don't leave tonight without receiving God's blessing. If you felt God for the first time, we invite you to come down and talk to the prayer team that's waiting for you."

Shane turned to me and said, "I think I want to go down there." I could only smile in bewilderment and accompany him on the first steps of his journey toward God.

That night, God answered my prayers in a big way. He convicted me of my own doubt and showed me just how efficient He can be! I realized that it's not up to me to decide when someone's heart is ready to receive God—but it *is* important that I pray with confidence and expectancy. I must continually decide to trust God for what is unseen and let Him guide the trajectory of my life in new and unexpected directions.

I am the LORD your God, who brought you up out of Egypt.
Open wide your mouth and I will fill it.
PSALM 81:10

"You of little faith," he said, "why did you doubt?"
MATTHEW 14: 31

Wisdom for the Week

DAY 1: PSALM 81:7-10
DAY 2: ECCLESIASTES 11:1-6
DAY 3: MATTHEW 7:7-12
DAY 4: PSALM 66:16-20
DAY 5: MATTHEW 17:15-20

Recommended Reading on Apologetics

Living Loud: Defending Your Faith by Norman Geisler and Joseph
   Holden (Nashville, TN: Broadman and Holman, 2000) equips
   students to confidently affirm their faith even in an indifferent or hostile environment.

Mere Christianity by C. S. Lewis (London: G. Bles, 1952) is a classic volume on the Christian faith. Based on lectures Lewis
   first presented on the radio, the book offers his reasons for
   belief in the gospel of Christ.

More Than a Carpenter by Josh McDowell (Wheaton, IL: Tyndale
   House Publishers, 1977) chronicles the author's own search
   for faith. The work offers an accessible discussion of Jesus
   Christ and the skeptics' questions.

Christ Among Other Gods by Erwin W. Lutzer (Chicago: Moody
   Press, 1994) contains 12 chapters that examine Jesus Christ
   compared to other religious figures such as Buddha, Krishna
   and Mohammed.

Philosophical Foundations for a Christian Worldview by J. P. Moreland
   and William Lane Craig (Downers Grove, IL: InterVarsity
   Press, 2003). Two philosophers' takes on issues of reality and
   eternity, time and space, faith and skepticism.

Defending Your Faith: An Introduction to Apologetics by R. C. Sproul
   (Wheaton, IL: Crossway Books, 2003) presents four "prin-
   ciples of knowledge" and follows with an examination of
   the existence for God and with various considerations for
   faith in Jesus Christ.

The Case for Christ by Lee Strobel (Grand Rapids, MI: Zondervan,
   1999) presents arguments about the accuracy of Scripture.
   The chapters contain discussions with experts who address
   the author's various doubts about Jesus and the Bible.

22

Under God's Roof

Believing the Father Will Meet My Needs

By Leah Danielle Robin, Whitworth College

And my God will meet all your needs according to his
glorious riches in Christ Jesus.
PHILIPPIANS 4:19

I opened up my sock drawer on a Friday morning. Emptiness
stared back at me. Despite the brand-spanking-new package of
white Hansen socks I purchased before fall classes began, my
sock supply had steadily decreased with each round of laundry.
Whether my socks were being stolen or the college dryers were
eating them was a mystery, but I was late for class and defi-
nitely out of socks. I slipped into a pair of flip-flops and ran out
the door into a cold rain.

My no-sock problem was just the latest entry on my long
list of concerns since starting college. My shampoo, ink car-
tridge, stationery and stock of snacks were all quickly dimin-
ishing. And since I was no longer living at home, I couldn't
casually inform my mom that I needed a new bottle of Herbal
Essence or ask my dad to pick up some ink the next time he
was at Staples.

I worried about not being able to afford the items I needed.
Washing my hair and printing out essays were vital elements
of my life! My lack of money seemed overwhelming, but God

would soon show Himself to me as my Father. He would take care of me in every way.

That next Tuesday morning, an unexpected knock came on my dorm-room door. "I was cleaning out my closet," my friend told me, holding out a grocery bag. "I've never worn these. Hope you can use them." The bag was stuffed with new socks.

Later that afternoon, a printer showed up in our dorm lobby with a note attached: "Free. Please take me." Next to the printer was an unused package of ink cartridges.

Before the day was over, another friend gave me a wrapped gift and a card. I tore open the gift wrap to find a beautiful box of stationery.

I was overwhelmed by God's goodness, and I immediately thought of the verse that tells us He is "a father to the fatherless" (Psalm 68:5). Since I no longer live under the roof of my earthly father, God has revealed Himself to me as *Abba*, my Daddy. I can truly trust Him to take care of me, even with the little things. Sockless days no longer produce panic, but rather a smile. My Daddy will pull through.

Wisdom for the Week

DAY 1: PSALM 50:14-23
DAY 2: PSALM 68:1-6
DAY 3: PSALM 9:17-18
DAY 4: PSALM 72:4-7
DAY 5: ACTS 5:29-35

Students and Credit Cards

Don't be bamboozled by tempting credit-card offers. Plastic cash can carry a big price tag. Use discretion and avoid needless debt.

- Use credit cards for necessities, such as buying books and other school items—not for buying fast food or movie tickets.

- Don't charge more than you can pay when the bill is due at the end of the month. Remember: Each time you use your card, you are getting a short-term loan.

- Avoid using credit cards when you are feeling disappointed and discouraged or celebratory and impulsive.

- Never use your credit card to get a cash advance. Borrow from friends or family instead.

- Check the card company's policies about fees, interest rates, spending limits and late-payment penalties. Avoid cards with annual fees.

- Keep credit-card company information in a safe place so that you can contact them quickly if your card is lost or stolen.

- Examine monthly credit-card statements to guard against unauthorized charges or unexpected fees.

- Consider using prepaid gift or debit cards as safer alternatives to credit cards.

- If you really need a credit card, choose one with bonus options, such as cash discounts or airline miles. Get the most for your money.

23

Giving Thanks

Counting My Blessings

By Melissa Lilley, Campbell University

*It is good to praise the LORD and make music to your name,
O Most High, to proclaim your love in the morning
and your faithfulness at night.*

PSALM 92:1-2

During my summer internship, the staff circulated prayer requests through email. Sometimes the requests were personal—a family member diagnosed with cancer or a friend recovering from a stroke. Other times the pleas for prayer traveled great distances, such as a missionary in South America whose daughter was kidnapped. My first reaction was to skim the text and move on, but as the requests popped up in my inbox, my heart was turned.

I was reminded of just how much I have to be thankful for. Sadly, it's rare that I offer a prayer of thanksgiving rather than a prayer of "Give me" or "Here's my problem; let's fix it now." As I jotted down all I had to be thankful for, it was not long before I wondered why I worried so much, why I complained so often. Perhaps taking a look at a few items from my list will help jog your memory about some of your own blessings.

I often feel swamped with work, with no clue how I will ever get it all done, but I have been blessed with a healthy mind able to learn and study. I'm thankful for the computer that I'm composing this essay on, and that I can do so in the comfort of my apartment.

I have my health. I complain when my year-round allergies go nuts, but it's been awhile since I've battled the flu or been really sick. And after living with asthma, seeing my dad escape a health scare and watching my pastor's wife lose her two-year battle with cancer, I don't take for granted each morning I wake up feeling good.

I am grateful for my family. Yes, my parents tell me to call them so that they'll know I got home safely, and they always remind me to get my flu shot—but from this I know they love me. I grin when my sister calls—especially when it's just to talk and not to inform me about the clothes she borrowed from my closet that week.

I'm thankful for my church family. Friends bless my life daily, and I thank God I don't have to be on this journey alone. I am thankful for the freedom I have to worship where I choose and to live in a country where so many of my freedoms are protected.

I'm thankful for little pleasures: sitting in the fourth row of the Dean Dome to cheer on the Tarheels, buying a new CD and unwrapping it before I leave the parking lot, getting a phone call from my best friend, finding time to share a meal with my roommates.

I'm thankful that Jesus not only forgives me when I fail to look gratefully to the heavens but that He's also promised always to be by my side.

For all this and more, I am thankful. What about you?

Wisdom for the Week

DAY 1: PSALM 116:16-19
DAY 2: EPHESIANS 5:15-20
DAY 3: DANIEL 2:17-23
DAY 4: 2 CORINTHIANS 9:6-11
DAY 5: JOHN 11:38-43

Let's Talk Turkey

Turkey describes more than the bird with the ample bosom used as the centerpiece on most American dinner tables every Thanksgiving. "Turkey" is also a slang term to label endeavors that failed spectacularly. The term has become a popular tag for bombs, losers and bad ideas. Here are a few turkeys of the recent and not-so-recent past.

Automobiles
Ford Edsel (1958-60)
Yugo (1986-92)

Christmas Song
"Grandma Got Run Over by a Reindeer" (1984)

Hairstyles
Mullet, Mohawk

Inventions
Landmines, Car Alarms

Math Problem
Kato's Conjecture (took more than 40 years to solve)

Movies
From Justin to Kelly (2003)
Plan 9 from Outer Space (1959)

Television Programs
Reality shows
Car 54, Where Are You? (1961-63)

Pets
Chia Pets, Pet Rocks

Toys
Cabbage Patch Kids
Beanie Babies

Sports Mascot
Artie the Artichoke

Sidewalk Chicken

Stepping Aside in Humility

By James G. Finney, Dartmouth College

Therefore, as God's chosen people, holy and dearly loved, clothe yourselves with compassion, kindness, humility, gentleness and patience.

COLOSSIANS 3:12

Have you ever played sidewalk chicken? Someone is walking directly toward you and one of you must step aside, or you will collide. Sometimes you're the one who gives in and moves. Sometimes you plow straight ahead, willing to crash into the other person if he or she does not step out of your way.

A lot of life is a game of relational chicken. In arguments with roommates or friends, ask yourself, *Do I give in to their needs or charge ahead until I get my way?* It's a fight between pride and humility: Do you fight for your own way out of pride, or do you humbly look out for the needs of others?

Humility sounds great in theory, but how can we possibly stay humble in daily life? Even the most seasoned follower of Christ struggles to step aside and let the other person pass. My pride really comes out when I'm driving. When someone cuts me off, I usually feel haughty and offended. I think, *How dare he!* The truth is, I've done it to others countless times myself. Thanking God for His protection and grace when I've cut other people off takes care of my own pride.

The expression of humility in my life is entirely a response to Christ's humility. Philippians 2:8 says that I should have the same attitude as Jesus because "being found in appearance as a man, he humbled himself and became obedient to death—even death on a cross!" The only way believers can be humble is to see Christ's humility and recognize their own humble positions as debtors before God. The key to a humble life is to respond appropriately to Jesus' sacrifice.

What is this appropriate response? First Thessalonians 5:18 says to "give thanks in all circumstances, for this is God's will for you in Christ Jesus." Gratitude places us in a position of dependence. Being grateful to God for everything makes us recognize that our talents, gifts and blessings are His provisions. Pride, on the other hand, compels us to believe we are good, talented and important—that we own the whole sidewalk. If we are grateful for everything—for the shoes we walk in, the pavement we stroll on and all our fellow pedestrians—we recognize that any good in us is purely a gift from Him. In gratitude to God we will find it difficult to treat others with pride. In everything, thank God, and in this our hearts will be humble.

Wisdom for the Week

Day 1: Proverbs 3:13-26

Day 2: Ephesians 4:1-8

Day 3: James 4:1-10

Day 4: Proverbs 22:1-6

Day 5: Proverbs 11:2-12

Pondering Pride

Proverbs 16:18 says, "Pride goes before destruction, a haughty spirit before a fall." Here are some additional wise words about pride:

- "Sweet praise is like perfume. It's fine if you don't swallow it." (Dwight D. Eisenhower)

- "Get rid of the idea that we understand ourselves; it is the last conceit to go." (Oswald Chambers, *My Utmost for His Highest*)

- "A proud man is always looking down on things and people; and, of course, as long as you're looking down, you can't see something that's above you." (C. S. Lewis, *Mere Christianity*)

- "God sends no one away empty except those who are full of themselves." (Dwight L. Moody)

- "Of all the causes which conspire to blind Man's erring judgment, and misguide the mind, What the weak head with strongest bias rules, Is pride, the never-failing vice of fools." (Alexander Pope, *An Essay on Criticism,* Part 2, lines 201-204)

- "Temper is what gets most of us into trouble. Pride is what keeps us there." (Mark Twain)

25

Lean on Me

Rejecting Self-Sufficiency

By Hannah Naomi Pizelo, Biola University

*May the God who gives endurance and encouragement
give you a spirit of unity among yourselves as you follow Christ Jesus.*

ROMANS 15:5

I marched into my dorm room one day to find my roommate's furniture rearranged. Her television stand was in the middle of the room with the ugly back of the TV facing my side. I glared at her. She didn't seem to notice, so as I began getting ready for bed, I made extra noise to let her know I wasn't happy.

She *still* didn't notice.

Her obliviousness made me even more furious. Finally I burst out, "You should have asked me before you rearranged your furniture!"

She looked at me, stunned.

"I don't want this ugly back of the TV with all the cords and junk facing me!" I shouted. Before I knew it, we were fighting like hungry cats over a goldfish. Sure, we were quarreling over a small matter; but as our quarrel escalated, I found myself bringing up many other offenses that upset me—little details here and there that had built up over the weeks.

That fight eventually turned into one of the best conversations I ever had with my roommate. The great thing she did for me was talk through every issue and complaint I had. She gave me a chance to start clean. I realized that night—about a month into the school year—that I couldn't go around acting like Ms. Social all the time, always wearing a plastic smile and ready with a glib answer to the question "How are you doing?" No one expected me to be perfect and composed at all times. I would have more stupid-TV-stand days when the pressures of life got to me. I needed to draw close to people who would understand so that when I *did* explode, they would be there to talk me through it.

Now I try to express my feelings and react honestly with my friends. I need them to see me as I am, and I sometimes need to talk through some conflicts so that I don't fly off the handle. I am in a new season of my life, different from where I've ever been, and I need some extra support—as do my friends.

As you enter your new college world, don't trivialize the changes you are going through. Be open with those around you. You will need their support. It's so easy to play the "island," pretending to be independent and to have it all together. Looking self-sufficient feels good at first, but you'll need help through what is ahead. When you have *your* stupid-TV-stand days (and you will!), you won't feel so alone if you've taken time to foster honest friendships. You'll be able to draw on the strength of others.

Wisdom for the Week

DAY 1: 1 CORINTHIANS 1:10-18

DAY 2: PHILIPPIANS 2:1-11

DAY 3: PSALM 133

DAY 4: 2 TIMOTHY 3:14-17

DAY 5: ACTS 2:42-47

Tips for Staying Awake

- **Dress up.** If you look nice, you won't feel like you ought to be in bed.

- **Take a sprint down the hall.** Getting your body moving wakes you up.

- **In class, hold your pen vertically over your lap** when you're not busy taking notes. If you start to doze, the pen will drop and wake you up.

- **Eat chocolate-covered espresso beans.** You can take them with you everywhere.

- **Suck on peppermints** or any type of lozenge with menthol. As the menthol clears your airways, your mind will feel clearer too.

- **In class, focus on stretching and flexing each part of your body,** starting with your toes and slowly working your way to your neck and head.

- **Work in spaces that don't accommodate naps.** Stay away from couches, beds and places where you are completely alone.

- **Take time to engage socially.** Even though you may be feeling dazed, smiling or exchanging a few words with another person will make you feel conscious.

- **Change your routine.** Walk a different route to class. Listen to music that's not familiar to you.

—Rebecca Pearsey, Biola University

26

The Work of Your Hands

Seeing the Wonders of Creation

By Davina Choy, Biola University

When I consider your heavens, the work of your fingers, the moon and the stars, which you have set in place, what is man that you are mindful of him, the son of man that you care for him?

PSALM 8:3-4

Nothing could dampen my preteen enthusiasm for winter camp—not the dizzying roads that led up into the mountains, not the wormy looking outhouse, not our windowless cabin that rained down dust on us from the ceiling.

Our cabin was near the edge of a cliff that overlooked a lake. The view was unlike anything I'd ever seen: sun on the water, a breeze ruffling the trees, brilliant white clouds scudding across the sky. The moment I first saw the view, I knew without a doubt that God existed and was good and perfect above everyone and everything. From that day on, I woke at the crack of dawn just to see the sunrise.

I'd never before been so touched by nature. I found myself noticing and appreciating things I'd previously overlooked. It made me want to read the Bible and want to *know* God. I needed to know what it meant to have a relationship with the Creator—the One who made the fuzzy black bear we'd seen wandering around camp at night, the One who formed the tiny speckled sparrow that scurried around our porch.

On the last night of camp after everyone else trudged, bleary-eyed, back to their cabins after campfire worship, I lay on a smooth rock and was amazed at how bright and alive the stars were above me. I spent almost an hour just staring in silence at the sky. I was struck with complete awe at how vast the heavens seemed and how small and insignificant I felt—just an onlooker. I was hit with an overwhelming desire to fly, to jump off the edge of the cliff and sail into the dark unknown. (I didn't, of course.)

That night sky was an epiphany. It made me see God in a different light. He wasn't just the God that I prayed to for good birthday presents and faster healing for my scabs. This was the God who made the heavens and the earth! Never before had that phrase held so much meaning. I realized how great and powerful the Lord is, and I reveled in His love. I was a wretched girl on the brink of teenage rebellion, yet the Lord had let me experience His creation.

Perhaps it was the twinkling stars or the clean forest air, but that night I felt closer to God than ever before.

Wisdom for the Week

DAY 1: PSALM 136:1-9

DAY 2: PSALM 19:1-11

DAY 3: ISAIAH 45:7-12

DAY 4: GENESIS 1:1-5

DAY 5: ACTS 17:22-31

How to Handle the Stress of Finals Week

- **Remember that professors aren't out to fail you.** They want you to do well. The final exam will not be as difficult as you think. You know the material.

- **Develop a rewards system for studying**: Set goals for yourself to study for a certain amount of time and reward yourself with something you enjoy.

- **Get enough sleep.** Try to get at least seven hours of sleep each night.

- **Don't be afraid to ask for help.** Asking for assistance will relieve the anxiety that comes from not understanding a particular concept.

- **Get a massage or a pedicure**, or participate in some other relaxing or stress-relieving activity.

- **Identify the source of your stress and take care of it.** If procrastination is increasing your worry, plan ahead. Get a friend to hold you accountable to deadlines.

- **Take breaks every now and again.** This will lead your thoughts away from finals and relieve your mind for a while.

- **Make time for God.** God will reward you in His own way for your faithfulness.

- **Realize that God has you in His plans.** The stress of finals week has a purpose, even if you're not sure at the moment what that purpose is.

—Ryan Newton, Biola University

No Walls

Trading My Good Works for Christ's Righteousness

By Hilary Reddick, Michigan State University

*Stand firm then . . . with the breastplate
of righteousness in place.*
EPHESIANS 6:14

Robert Frost's "Mending Wall" begins, "Something there is that doesn't love a wall."[1] I have built a beautiful wall of righteousness around my life, stacking up good works and trying hard not to make mistakes. Yet there's something in me that doesn't love a wall. I'll confess: Many times I've taken a stone off just to see how far I could throw it. Or I've rolled a boulder away just to test the balance of the other stones. Somehow my wall never stays intact.

I remember very clearly one Bible study I attended about a year ago. We were talking about righteousness, and we happened on the passage in Ephesians about the armor of God. It struck me that our righteousness as believers is not a wall. It is a breastplate. Consider the differences: A breastplate is one piece, made by God and stamped with His insignia. We don't mount it on our wall; we choose to put it on, to trust it to protect us. It takes a lot of faith to believe this smallish piece of metal will protect us better than our big, strong wall. It certainly doesn't hide us the way a wall does.

Paul says in Galatians 2:21, "I do not set aside the grace of God, for if righteousness could be gained through the law, Christ died for nothing!" I have experienced the guilt and insecurity of trusting my own crumbling, imperfect wall to protect me instead of trusting God's righteousness to cover my sin. But Ephesians 6:16 encourages me: "Take up the shield of faith, with which you can extinguish *all* the flaming arrows of the evil one" (emphasis added). I no longer need to fear failure—God's righteousness is sufficient.

Recently my biggest struggle with this issue has been to realize that God's righteousness is not only sufficient, but it also excludes all my other efforts. I often want to put on the breastplate and then stand behind my wall—just in case something too intimidating comes along. But that is not faith. In Philippians, Paul gives a long list of all his good works, but then he says, "I consider them rubbish, that I may gain Christ and be found in him" (Philippians 3:8). In view of grace, Paul's righteousness—his "wall"—was not only garbage, but it also kept him from knowing Christ and gaining His righteousness.

Wisdom for the Week

DAY 1: ROMANS 4:13-21

DAY 2: HEBREWS 4:10-16

DAY 3: DANIEL 3:13-27

DAY 4: JOHN 4:9-15

DAY 5: PROVERBS 28:18-28

Note

1. Robert Frost, "Mending Wall," published in Louis Untermeyer, ed., *Modern American Poetry* (New York: Harcourt, Brace and Howe, 1919; New York: Bartleby.com, 1999). http://www.bartleby.com/104/64.html.

Walls

Walls can serve as both physical and metaphorical barriers with the potential to either protect or isolate. They offer safety, promote contemplation, create frustration and command attention. Here are several particularly notable walls:

- **Berlin Wall**—built to keep people in. The first boundaries were made of barbed wire. Eventually, concrete walls standing about 12 feet high fortified the 96-mile barrier, which separated East and West Berlin.

- **Great Wall of China**—built to keep people out. The 4,000-mile wall dates from the fifth century B.C. It was first made of stones and earth, but bricks were added during the Ming Dynasty (A.D. 1368-1644).

- **Vietnam Veterans Memorial Wall**—built to remember people. The black granite panels, stretching about 493 feet, were constructed in 1982. Seventy sections, each 10 feet high, are inscribed with the names of 58,256 soldiers who served in the war.

- **Wall of Jericho**—built for protection. Joshua led the Israelites in a march that destroyed the wall around Jericho about 1410 B.C. (see Joshua 6).

- **Western Wall**—built as a place of worship (originally part of a wall of the Second Temple). The 43 rows of ancient stone extended about 187 feet in ancient times. Also known as the Wailing Wall, it is located on Jerusalem's Temple Mount, where people assemble daily for prayer.

Little Labels

Finding My Identity in Christ

By Jen Montzingo, Seattle Pacific University

Therefore if any man be in Christ, he is a new creature.
2 CORINTHIANS 5:17, *KJV*

After a long day at work, I am tired as I stand in line at my local grocery store with a friend. All I want is to make it out of the store and get on with life.

In front of me in line are a man and his little girl. "Look at that tiny woman," the girl squeals. Her father claps a hand over her mouth. The others in line are now staring, not only at me, but also at the small child who has caused all the commotion. Like an annoying song set on repeat, I think back to other life moments like this one. I can almost predict the questions that will soon follow this child's wide-eyed stare:

"Have you always been so small?"

"Can you drive?"

"Why were you born that way?"

I momentarily look at my friend, who rolls her eyes. She gives me her "can't people just get over it?" smirk. And so this turns into another educational moment for a stranger. I admit that, at times, it irritates me that I cannot just walk in and out of the grocery store like any normal person. I answer this young girl's questions politely, but I wish she and her father only knew how often I pray to be free from distractions like this.

When I walk into a room, I get noticed—at the age of 22, I am only a couple inches over four feet tall, officially diagnosed with achondroplasian dwarfism. This situation at the grocery store is not the first time I have been stopped for an "educational moment." My uncommon size inevitably attracts a great deal of natural curiosity. I understand the fascination with something so out of the ordinary; nonetheless, I long for others to realize there is more to me than my height.

Those of us who command attention, for one reason or another, must remember that we are more than what we are known for. Sometimes it feels hopeless. Sometimes it feels like I will never overcome the stereotype others have of me. But the hope I have of being seen and loved completely for who I am comes from a deep assurance that God promises to transform ashes into beauty.

The One who has all authority to label or condemn does neither. With Christ, every label was nailed to the cross. We now live in God's promises of a new identity. What hope! Etched in our minds and hearts are all the terms we have all been labeled with, but someday we will be able to completely slough off all our limiting labels and see ourselves the way Christ does.

Wisdom for the Week

DAY 1: 1 SAMUEL 16:1-13

DAY 2: 1 TIMOTHY 4:6-16

DAY 3: PSALM 86:11-17

DAY 4: EPHESIANS 1:1-12

DAY 5: MATTHEW 10:28-32

"New You" Resolutions

Perhaps you decide that this semester you'll improve yourself: You'll lose weight, study harder, attend more concerts or read more books—but why not make a different kind of resolution? Consider these suggestions:

- **Memorize a passage of Scripture.** The meaning of a passage really comes through when you commit it to memory. Volunteer to recite your memorized passage for your church worship service or Bible study group for a different and powerful form of worship!

- **Write notes of thanks or encouragement.** Personal notes are tangible sources of encouragement for recipients. Who doesn't love personal mail?

- **Take more pictures**. In 10 years, you'll be thrilled that you bothered to document your everyday life and take snapshots of all your friends in college. Don't forget to capture those midnight coffee and doughnut runs!

- **Turn your passion into a ministry.** Whatever your passion—music, art, organization skills—there is a place for you in ministry! Learn how you can use your talent to serve others at your school or local church.

- **Create a soundtrack of your life.** Capture the essence of your college years by creating a playlist of your favorite songs. Use the playlist to motivate yourself, lift your mood or keep you moving!

—Shannon Kooistra, Azusa Pacific University

29

Clockwork

Spending Time on What's Important

By Paul DeGoes, The Master's College

The length of our days is seventy years—or eighty,
if we have the strength; yet their span is but trouble and sorrow,
for they quickly pass, and we fly away.

PSALM 90:10

Time—who has enough of it? Especially we students, who are imposed on from all quarters by professors, friends, church, sports and so much else—all of which hungrily devour as much of our time as we're willing to part with.

Wouldn't it be nice if that old-school professor (yeah, the one everybody tries to avoid, but whose class you were unlucky enough to land this semester) would look kindly at you and say, "Oh, you're just putting too much time and effort into these assignments; you really must ease back!"? Ever hear your pastor tell you that you're spending too much time in prayer and the study of Scripture? Not on your life! It seems as though everyone we meet is ready and waiting to gobble up another piece of the pie, to take up another hour or two of what is already scarce as gold.

Twenty-four hours; that's it in a day. You have it, I have it, and the students next door do too. It's one of the few things I have in common with the president, with the woman pushing a shopping cart down the street and with every other living soul. No one gets more or less time in a day than anyone else.

The only difference is what we fill that time with—and we all fill it, one way or another.

I've never met a student, freshman to senior, who didn't have time—but I have met many who didn't have time *for* things. We spend time on what's important to us, what's worthwhile, what matters. Saying "I don't have time for that" is shorthand for "That doesn't mean enough to me to spend time on it." In a way, there is no truer test of what I care about than what I spend my 24 hours on.

It's really quite telling of my heart to realize how often I undervalue friends or family or church, all under the guise of not having time. It's not about *having* time; it's about what I choose to spend it on.

Who has time? We all do—for what matters to us.

Wisdom for the Week

DAY 1: PSALM 139:1-14

DAY 2: HEBREWS 10:19-25

DAY 3: 2 PETER 3:8-13

DAY 4: GALATIANS 4:4-7

DAY 5: PSALM 69:13-17

Tips for Time Management

- Organize your day or week by making a specific plan.

- Prioritize tasks by their importance, not their urgency.

- Avoid over-commitment; learn to say no and be firm about it.

- Make to-do lists and follow them.

- Be realistic when planning how much you can do in a day or week.

- Combine activities when possible. (For example, read an assignment while waiting for an appointment or study note cards while eating breakfast.)

- Perform difficult tasks when you are most alert.

- Shun procrastination.

- Begin working on complex assignments by doing the small sections that will eventually lead to completion of the entire project.

- Complete easy assignments or simple duties when you are feeling overwhelmed.

- Finish something. No matter how insignificant, it will give you a sense of control and accomplishment.

- Use time-draining activities (such as watching TV, playing computer games or talking with friends) as a reward for when you have completed other more essential tasks (such as homework).

30

Outer Shell

Keeping Up Appearances

By Kara Kennedy, Point Loma Nazarene University

So from now on we regard no one from a worldly point of view.
Though we once regarded Christ in this way, we do so no longer.
Therefore, if anyone is in Christ, he is a new creation;
the old has gone, the new has come!
2 CORINTHIANS 5:16-17

I don't remember what day it was that my morning routine went beyond dressing, eating breakfast and brushing my teeth, but somewhere along the line, I started feeling the need to make every aspect of myself as perfect as I could before I left my room.

My concern about my appearance intensified during eighth grade. Three months after getting braces, my facial structure began to misalign. Doctors told me I would need surgery if I ever wanted to look "normal" again. Thus began a self-consciousness that grew worse every year, until by my senior year all I could think about was how much I hated my appearance and how much better my life would be if only I looked like everybody else. I disengaged from having a social life and buried myself in academic work, never letting myself become too attached or sharing too much of myself with anyone.

I could not have corrective surgery until I turned 18, and then I had to wait until my braces came off. By that time I had already started college—although I seriously considered postponing my education until I thought I looked better. Blame it on culture, the media or my peers, but I wanted so desperately to look good that I didn't even care about the risks involved with major surgery. I had the operation as soon as school let out for Christmas break, not mentioning my plans to my college friends.

When I returned to school a week after the spring semester began, I was extremely nervous, terrified of what people would think of my post-surgery face. Yet to my surprise, no one said a word. My friends simply showered me with hugs and greetings and said they had missed me. Only my roommate said I looked "different." Her warmth and acceptance allowed me to explain about the surgery.

I soon realized that I had underestimated my friends' compassion. I realized that my roommate and other friends were godly people who truly did care for me, no matter how I looked.

Our culture puts too much value on physical beauty. I realize now that I let these superficial ideas undermine and nearly destroy me. Why else would I have wasted so many years in self-loathing and social isolation? When I needed comfort and acceptance, God provided people who genuinely cared for me, which restored my faith in close personal relationships.

After the surgery, my confidence grew and my personality blossomed, not only because I was no longer paranoid about how horrible I looked but also because God showed me I could trust my friends. Their unconditional acceptance allowed me to abandon my defiant me-against-the-world attitude.

Wisdom for the Week

DAY 1: EPHESIANS 1:18-23
DAY 2: PSALM 86:1-7
DAY 3: JOHN 6:35-40
DAY 4: ISAIAH 64:5-9
DAY 5: PHILIPPIANS 1:3-6

How to Avoid the "Freshman 15"

Salad bar, dessert bar, drink bar—so many unlimited choices in the university dining hall can send your mind and appetite spinning. Before you know it, you'll be wearing those choices. Here are some tips for avoiding the dreaded "Freshman 15."

- Stay away from the French-fry line.

- Eat your veggies.

- Play intramural sports.

- Avoid midnight fast-food runs.

- Don't be a stranger in the fitness center.

- Avoid eating dessert at every meal.

- Fast occasionally and take walks with friends.

- Avoid late-night snacks.

- Don't keep junk food in your dorm room.

—Sarah Jensen, Biola University

31

Black Hours

Feeling God's Presence in Despair

By Jesse Ataide, Point Loma Nazarene University

My God, my God, why hast thou forsaken me?
MATTHEW 27:46, *KJV*

I silently cried out these same words one night from a small bed in a tiny dorm room in London. I had arrived in Britain's capital city as a study-abroad student just two weeks before and was beginning to feel the stresses of adjusting to life in a completely unfamiliar place.

Earlier that evening, I had received an email from an old friend of mine who also happened to be my ex-girlfriend. It was a mass email directed to our broad circle of mutual friends, and it contained a link to some pictures she had posted on the Internet of her new boyfriend. Months had passed since our breakup, and any feelings I had held for her had long since faded—that is, until I opened the webpage and looked at the photos.

The first thing I noticed was how strong a resemblance the new boyfriend had to somebody I knew: *me*. From the pictures, I gathered that we were about the same height and had the same brown eyes, brown hair and long sideburns. He was *me* in a sideways baseball cap. I was stunned. But that wasn't all I noticed. The look of happiness on my ex-girlfriend's face was obvious, especially to somebody who knew her smile well.

I left the Internet café that night in a daze, for now not only was I feeling disconnected from those in my life back home, but I also had a very strong impression of being completely forgotten, replaced in my absence by someone who strongly resembled me.

Two lines from Gerard Manley Hopkins's poem "I Wake and Feel the Fell of Dark, Not Day" perfectly capture what I felt that night as I tossed and turned on that too-short bed:

What hours, O what black hours we have spent
This night! what sights you, heart, saw; ways you went![1]

They were indeed black hours, some of the darkest I have ever experienced. The emotions I had repressed for months finally hit me with a painful fury, unmasking much larger issues I had long avoided. I realized in that moment that I had been stuck in a dead emotional state, comfortably numbed, so I couldn't feel any pain. At the same time, by avoiding pain, I had lost the capacity to feel joy.

After a long time, I began to direct my feelings of anger, resentment and loneliness toward God—and for the first time I honestly felt as if God was listening to me. It was a breakthrough in my faith, which had long been languishing in disrepair.

It's easy in a state of complete despair to feel that God is far away and simply doesn't care. Yet somehow, God faithfully reappears in the lowest moment, willing to demonstrate how the divine presence we yearned for had really been there the entire time.

Note

1. Gerard Manley Hopkins, *Poems* (London: Humphrey Milford, 1918; New York: Bartleby.com, 1999). http://www.bartleby.com/122/45.html.

Wisdom for the Week

DAY 1: HEBREWS 11:1-6

DAY 2: ACTS 14:19-22

DAY 3: PSALM 119:89-96

DAY 4: 1 KINGS 8:56-61

DAY 5: PSALM 89:5-8

Ten Things to Do When You're Feeling Lonely

1. Take a 20-minute walk and pray for everyone you know.

2. Do a kind deed for someone else.

3. Go to the campus fitness center and work out for 30 minutes.

4. Call a family member or a friend just to say hello. Refrain from whining.

5. Help a fellow student with homework or start working on an upcoming assignment.

6. Watch a madcap comedy like *Rat Race*, *A Fish Called Wanda* or something equally silly.

7. Write an old-fashioned pen-and-paper letter to a person you care about.

8. Get a disposable camera and take photographs of anything that pleases you.

9. Go to the library and read an interesting magazine.

10. Email messages to friends and family.

The Return of the Light

Traveling Through Darkness Toward Jesus

By Hillary Prag, Seattle Pacific University

The people walking in darkness have seen a great light;
on those living in the land of the shadow of death a light has dawned.
ISAIAH 9:2

Ancient Celtic Christians celebrated Christmas as the return of the light. Today, on the tiny Scottish island of Iona, it is still celebrated this way, though it is windy, cold and dark most of the day in the weeks surrounding Christmas.

Each summer, Iona is a destination for thousands of pilgrims who seek to connect with an ancient faith tradition. Visitors file silently through the crumbling nunnery, abbey and cemetery, cooled by a fresh sea breeze under a gentle sky. Then, as the last of the summer ferries are shuttled back across the sound, the local villagers begin boarding up their windows for the harsh winter. At Christmastime, it will be dark on the island by 4:30 in the afternoon, and it will not be light again until 9:30 in the morning.

The locals call this time of abbreviated light a "fertile darkness," and though it is oppressive, it is celebrated because the villagers know that things are still growing in the cold.

A woman I know from Iona says that people don't go outside their cozy homes into the winter darkness unless it is completely necessary. If they were to venture into the cold, the only objects visible would be the porch light of their nearest neighbor down the road. The fertile darkness throws its cloak over the island at night.

We, as lonely travelers in the dark, know a similar cold. We know what it is like to see only a feeble porch light in the distance and to trudge toward it with eager hope for what it might mean. The journey toward Christmas is a pilgrimage to the place where light returns to our lives.

We are not the only travelers on this path. The ancient Magi knew it well. The shepherds left their flocks for it. Pilgrims throughout history have left their places of security to journey toward a land where they hoped to find God. Yet travelers are surprised when they realize that God has come to meet them on that road and that He plans to journey with them the remainder of the way.

The story of Christmas is the story of the return of the light—a story of God sending Someone to walk this road with us. This is our assurance: We move toward the place where light returns to our path with great confidence in our fearless Guide.

> *Let the darkness of night surround us,*
> *Let light and warmth gather us*
> *And let God's people say Amen. . . .*
> *Let winds blow wild around us,*
> *But let hearts be glad and minds be calm*
> *And let God's people say Amen.*
> FROM *THE IONA COMMUNITY WORSHIP BOOK*[1]

Note

1. *The Iona Community Worship Book* (Iona: Wild Goose Publications, 1988).

Wisdom for the Week

DAY 1: JOHN 8:12-18

DAY 2: LUKE 5:13-16

DAY 3: LUKE 2:25-32

DAY 4: REVELATION 21:22-27

DAY 5: PSALM 43:2-5

Hollywood Holidays

Here are some old and new holiday movies to get you in the Christmas spirit.

- *Holiday Inn* (1942)

- *It's a Wonderful Life* (1946)

- *White Christmas* (1954)

- *A Charlie Brown Christmas* (1965)

- *A Christmas Story* (1983)

- *National Lampoon's Christmas Vacation* (1989)

- *Home Alone* (1990)

- *The Nightmare Before Christmas* (1993)

- *The Santa Claus* (1994)

- *Jingle All the Way* (1996)

- *Elf* (2003)

Thoughts from a Dorm Hallway

Hurting and Rejected by Roommates

By Brooke James, Biola University

A gentle answer turns away wrath, but a harsh word stirs up anger.
PROVERBS 15:1

Dorm life is not always what it's cracked up to be. At home, my sister and I shared a room and a wonderful relationship; but at college, meshing my life with two other freshmen was much more difficult.

My roommates and I had little in common, and our differences soon created a thick, unspoken tension. Eventually, they insisted I move out. They proposed that at the end of the fall semester, I trade rooms with their new best friend—an arrangement that would send me to live with strangers for the spring term.

Though hurt, rejected and frustrated, I agreed.

Then, the week before final exams and Christmas break, I came back to the dorm to find all my belongings in the middle of the hallway. I couldn't believe it! I just stood there crying. I had to be at a formal Christmas party in less than an hour, but getting ready was impossible with my belongings strewn everywhere.

None of the residence assistants came to my rescue. And when I objected to having my possessions dumped out in the hallway, my former roommates insisted I was being completely selfish for not moving sooner—and that I needed to get the rest of my stuff out so that their friend could settle in.

Responding in a Christian manner to my roommates proved to be a challenge. While I was still struggling with the situation, I was reminded of a verse card that a friend had left on my desk: Proverbs 15:1.

I knew my own gossip and complaints had contributed to the trouble I was in, but I also knew that I was being wronged unjustly. God's reminder to speak gently helped me to stand up for myself and still extend grace and forgiveness to my former roommates.

God calls His children to respond with gentleness rather than anger, even in the face of thoughtlessness and injustice. When the days are long and the words are harsh, speak gently and surprise others with kindness.

Wisdom for the Week

DAY 1: TITUS 3:3-8
DAY 2: PSALM 84:1-9
DAY 3: PSALM 120:1-7
DAY 4: 1 PETER 3:8-12
DAY 5: PROVERBS 15:4-7

Tips for Finding Christmas Spirit

- Read the Christmas story from Luke 2.

- Wear red and green and call out "Merry Christmas" every chance you get.

- Decorate your room. Include scents of cinnamon or evergreen.

- Play Christmas music.

- Get an old-fashioned Advent calendar to count down the days.

- Send homemade Christmas cards to your friends and family.

- Attend free Christmas concerts on campus or in local churches or civic auditoriums.

- Go caroling.

- Ask a professor if you can come to his or her home and bake Christmas cookies.

- Visit some community nativity scenes, or watch a local Christmas parade.

- Go out of your way to drive down that street where all the houses have lights.

- Make Santa Shakes by blending equal parts peppermint ice cream, milk and eggnog.

Her Last Morning

Treasuring the Present Moment

By Ashley Akins, Azusa Pacific University

Therefore do not worry about tomorrow, for tomorrow will worry about itself. Each day has enough trouble of its own.
MATTHEW 6:34

When I got to college, I often found myself counting the weeks until the end of the semester or even crossing off the days until the weekend. Sometimes I just couldn't wait to get through the day. When I felt stress about everything I had to get done, I automatically wished it was all over—and I kept looking to that future moment when I could finally relax.

During the second semester of my freshman year, one of the other freshmen girls from my university was killed in a horrible car accident.

I didn't really know her, but her death had a profound effect on me. I realized that when she woke up that morning, she had no idea it was going to be her last day on Earth. She didn't know that in a few hours she would be with her Savior.

I recalled what I had been thinking that same morning when I woke up, and I was mortified. If I had been in her place, my last day of life would have started with the thought, *I wish today was over because I really don't want to take that chemistry test. But only a few more hours and* then *things will be good.*

I wish my thoughts had been, *Thank You, Lord, for another day. I wonder what You have in store for me.* But they weren't, and that convicted me.

My failure to appreciate the present was deeply troubling. I realized that God wants to use me in every present moment— not tomorrow, not next week, not at the end of the semester. Worrying about the future robs me of the joy of today.

I'm learning it is better to replace my worry time each day with prayer. Paul wrote:

Do not be anxious about anything, but in everything, by prayer and petition, with thanksgiving, present your requests to God.
PHILIPPIANS 4:6

Wisdom for the Week

DAY 1: PSALM 46:1-10

DAY 2: 2 CORINTHIANS 4:6-18

DAY 3: ISAIAH 26:1-9

DAY 4: PROVERBS 56:3-9

DAY 5: JAMES 4:3-17

Carpe Diem, Anyone?

Carpe diem is the Latin phrase meaning "seize the day." The idea was extolled in the 1989 film *Dead Poets Society*, in which a teacher played by actor Robin Williams urges his students to resist conformity. The concept holds universal appeal. A quick Internet search reveals the far-reaching allure of seizing the day.

Scholarships
The Carpe Diem Foundation offers scholarships to students interested in improving "the quality of human life." For information and applications, see www.carpediemfoundation.org.

Movies
"Carpe Diem, A Dead Poets Society Page" contains links to the film *Dead Poets Society* and related topics. Lovers of the film can connect at www.geocities.com/CollegePark/5552/dps.htm.

Music
Carpe Diem is a German music company that offers an array of musical works from early music to classic and contemporary. You may place your orders at www.carpediem-records.com.

Food
Carpe Diem is a restaurant and lounge in Charlotte, North Carolina. Get a preview at www.carpediemrestaurant.com.

Horses
Carpe Diem Farm breeds classic Iberian (Lusitano) horses in Troy, Oregon. Have a look-see at www.carpe-diem-farm.com.

Travel
Carpe Diem Travel Ltd. specializes in tours to Cambodia and Laos. Book your trip at www.carpe-diem-travel.com.

Constant, Consistent, Continual

Taking Joy in the Reign of God

By Cassidy Hall, Iowa State University

Jesus Christ is the same yesterday and today and forever.
HEBREWS 13:8

It wasn't just another game: It was one of the best opportunities of the season. We were playing the team ranked twelfth in the nation, and we were ranked fourteenth. It was a great chance to prove ourselves—to show we were truly meant to be in the top 20, among the country's most elite teams. And being the underdogs, we had nothing to lose.

Before the game began, just like for every other game, some of the girls on our basketball team got together and prayed— not that we would win, but that God would be glorified in all we said and did.

For the first 20 minutes, the game was close. By halftime, the score was nearly tied. Yet when we came out on the court for the second half, victory slipped away from us. We didn't play the way we knew we could. We couldn't keep it consistent. We couldn't find our groove.

We lost by nearly 30 points in a game that felt like it might never end. I talked to God throughout that second half. He taught me some amazing truths as I sat in the quietness of His presence, in the midst of that deafening, rowdy gymnasium crowd. He pressed on my heart the truth of His constant reign over all things. As the final buzzer sounded to end this disappointing game, joy was still deeply rooted in my heart with the knowledge of God's constant and consistent authority.

Sometimes I picture God's constancy as a big statue, like the ones we have around campus—steady, strong, still. But God is not like a statue. Our God is in a constant state of motion, a constant state of loving us as daughters and sons, a constant state of pouring out grace, a constant state of changing and sustaining hearts.

Throughout all situations in our lives—our highs and lows, our wins and devastating losses—God never changes. He is constantly and consistently moving for His kingdom. He moves so that we might move to bring Him glory and delight.

We are called to take comfort in God's control, authority and reign over our lives—even during the most disappointing times. This is God's sovereignty, His perpetual motion. God is not and never will be still, but He will always be constant, consistent and continual in His movement.

Wisdom for the Week

DAY 1: PSALM 102:12-28

DAY 2: JAMES 1:16-18

DAY 3: MALACHI 3:6-7,16-18

DAY 4: HEBREWS 13:8-16

DAY 5: HEBREWS 7:23-28

Hail to the Chief

Presidential trivia is not just for political science majors. Try your hand at some trivia about the lesser-known facts about the residents of 1600 Pennsylvania Avenue.

1. Lincoln was the tallest president, but who was shortest?

2. Who was the only bachelor president?

3. Which president won a Pulitzer Prize?

4. Which president held an earned PhD?

5. Which president was born on July 4th?

6. Which presidents died on July 4th?

7. Which president wrote a book titled *George Washington*?

8. Which president learned English as a second language?

9. Which president's middle initial didn't stand for anything?

10. Which president had a candy bar named after his daughter?

11. Which president got expelled from college?

12. Which president once filed a UFO report?

13. Which president played semi-professional baseball?

14. Which president made Elvis Presley a "Federal Agent at Large"?

—Heather Buchanan, Chapman University

Answers: (1) Madison—at 5′4″; (2) Buchanan; (3) Kennedy; (4) Wilson; (5) Coolidge; (6) Jefferson, John Adams, Monroe; (7) Wilson; (8) Van Buren—he grew up speaking Dutch; (9) Truman; (10) Cleveland—according to its maker, the Baby Ruth bar was named for his daughter, Ruth; (11) Buchanan—he later returned and graduated; (12) Carter; (13) Eisenhower; (14) Nixon.

Taking the Plunge

Resting in the Fear of the Lord

By Sarah Schwartzendruber Shaffer, Taylor University

Tune your ears to wisdom, and concentrate on understanding.
Cry out for insight and understanding. Search for them as you would
for lost money or hidden treasure. Then you will understand what it
means to fear the LORD, and you will gain knowledge of God.
PROVERBS 2:2-5, NLT

As college students, our occupation is the pursuit of knowledge. We attend classes, take reams of notes, study late into the night—just to get through a class. With such responsibilities, how can we *concentrate*, *cry out* and *search* for godly insight? Wisdom is a far cry from the kind of knowledge we cram into our brains every day and forget as soon as we spill it back out in the form of tests and papers. We should pursue godly knowledge and wisdom aggressively.

I often start down the mental path of pursuing understanding, but as soon as the ideas get complex, I have trouble organizing them in my mind. Flustered, I throw the whole thing out. Proverbs 2:2-5 challenges me not to give up. It also encourages me to see that acknowledging my perplexity is actually a step toward wisdom and the fear of the Lord.

I had always wondered how searching for wisdom and understanding could give me a deeper concept of the fear of the

Lord. This is how: The more we pursue knowledge, the more we come to realize just how much we don't understand, how impossible it is to piece together all the snippets of understanding humanity has attained. The more I grasp how much there is to know, the more I realize how feeble I am in mind and spirit. The more I see the grand chasm between all human understanding and God's perfect, complete perspective, the more I respect Him and hold Him in awe.

Ironically, the more we realize that a chasm exists—and the larger we realize it to be—the closer we are to God. An analogy might help: The farther from the edge of the Grand Canyon a tourist is, the less the marvelous breadth of the canyon is realized, and the farther the tourist is from the other side. But if he or she boldly comes right up to the edge, maybe even descends a path into it, the more the tourist realizes just how grand the canyon is—and the closer the tourist is to reaching—and hearing from—the other side.

We and our simplemindedness are on one side; God and His perfect understanding are on the other. Let's step up to the edge of knowledge, pursue it without fear of the unknowable, and cup our ears to hear from the other side. As diligent students of God's Word, the deeper in we go, the closer we move to God.

Wisdom for the Week

DAY 1: PSALM 111

DAY 2: MATTHEW 7:24-29

DAY 3: DANIEL 12:3-4,10

DAY 4: PSALM 125

DAY 5: PROVERBS 8:10-21

Top Summer Jobs for College Students

1. Lifeguard at local pools, the YMCA or beaches

2. Counselor for youth camp, summer day camp, or local parks and recreation departments

3. Coach or referee in youth sports leagues

4. Tour guide for local museums, historical attractions or campus admissions department

5. Youth ministry intern or intern for business related to major field of study

6. Landscaper or lawn care technician for neighborhoods or local businesses

7. Tutor in a learning center or freelance

8. Auto detailer freelance or for a local body shop

9. Coffee shop or retail clerk in local businesses, grocery store chains or roadside stands

10. Restaurant servers in establishments that offer opportunities to earn tips

11. Dog sitter/walker for local pet owners or kennels

12. English language instructor in second-language programs or overseas

A Firm Rock Amid Waves

Safe in the Hands of Jesus

By Schuyler Ejay Eastin, Jr., Point Loma Nazarene University

"Lord if it's you," Peter replied, "tell me to come to you on the water."
"Come," he said. Then Peter got down out of the boat, walked on the
water and came toward Jesus. But when he saw the wind, he was
afraid and, beginning to sink, cried out, "Lord, save me!" Immediately
Jesus reached out his hand and caught him. "You of little faith,"
he said, "why did you doubt?"
MATTHEW 14:28-31

It is rare that many of us have to deal with death, especially at our relatively young ages. It is even rarer that a suicide touches our community. Most of us have no idea how to make sense of such a heartbreaking event. We wonder what amount of unfathomable inner despair would have brought someone we know to resort to such a devastating act.

During spring break of my junior year, one of my fellow students ended his life. His name was Chace, and I can't say that I was very close to him—but I had been in close enough proximity to him for those first three years of college to know there was great pain and also great brilliance beneath his quiet demeanor. He was the kind of acquaintance I had always expected to take an undefined but significant role in the background of my life—like one of those actors in the movies that you recognize but who never get the starring roles.

Only after Chace was gone did I start to realize the true weight of his seemingly insignificant comments, which tended to resound just off-center from my own daily focus. The words that had curled from his lips like a small plume of smoke began to glaze my eyes, and I was able to see—too late—that he was sinking, like Peter, into a cold, watery despair.

Now that Chace's seat in my Seventeenth-Century Literature class was forever empty, I wondered if I could have been the firm hand to help him back to safety. I might never have been close enough to Chace to really reach out to him, and I will never know if that hand of rescue could have been mine. Yet as I meditate on the pain my classmate must have felt, I recognize that there is a hand that will always be ready to steady or lift me completely out of any watery mire I may drift into.

As the poet John Milton wrote about the death of a friend,

Weep no more, woeful shepherds, weep no more,
For Lycidas, your sorrow, is not dead,
Sunk though he be beneath the watery floor: . . .
So Lycidas sunk low, but mounted high
Through the dear might of Him that walk'd the waves.[1]

The feet of Jesus will always walk the waves more steadily than any of ours, and His hands will never tire of pulling our soaked, despairing souls to safety.

Note

1. John Milton, "Lycidas: Elegy on a Friend Drowned in the Irish Channel," lines 165-67, 172-73, published in Francis Turner Palgrave, comp., *The Golden Treasury* (London: Macmillan, 1875; New York: Bartleby.com, 1999). www.bartleby.com/106/66.html.

Wisdom for the Week

DAY 1: 2 TIMOTHY 4:16-18
DAY 2: DANIEL 6:13-27
DAY 3: ACTS 5:17-24
DAY 4: NEHEMIAH 4:9-17
DAY 5: JOSHUA 1:1-9

Warning Signs of Suicide

Behavior Clues

- Becomes angry and aggressive or moody and quiet.
- Sleeps too much or too little; starts using drugs.
- Gains weight or skips meals and has little appetite.
- Gives away very personal or private possessions.
- Withdraws from normal or usual activities.

Conversation Clues

- Focuses on personal losses such as the death of friends or family members.
- Concentrates on individual failures and regrets.
- Admits a sense of powerlessness; talks about dying.
- Asks others to complete unfinished tasks or manage unresolved matters.

Ways to Help

- Listen to the person's concerns without offering judgment or opinions.
- Encourage the person to discuss his or her feelings, plans or fears, and do not leave him or her alone.
- Seek professional help from campus student services, even if the person refuses to seek help on his or her own.

38

Unbroken Hallelujahs

Delighting the Lord of Laughter and Song

By Naomi Spurrier Smith, Houghton College

The LORD your God is with you, he is mighty to save.
He will take great delight in you, he will quiet you with his love,
he will rejoice over you with singing.

ZEPHANIAH 3:17

I was in my dorm room one afternoon, reading quietly on my bed, when I heard faint strains of the "Hallelujah" chorus coming from somewhere nearby. I listened for a bit, and then, unable to suppress my curiosity, I tiptoed down the hallway and peeked in the open door of the room where the music was playing. On the floor lay two girls, fast asleep with their heads on their pillows, while the voices of the choir boomed out the last mighty round of hallelujahs. Grinning to myself, I hurried back to my room to laugh out loud.

Somehow the picture of those girls sleeping in the midst of a noisy, majestic song restored my weary spirits. Often, I struggle to remember that anyone—let alone the Lord—takes great delight in me. Most days all I see are my weaknesses, and my inability to do everything to the best of my ability bothers me. I want to have time to be a faithful friend and time to be a servant scholar; I want to have time to pray and time to work and time to have fun. Too many roles and responsibilities leave me overwhelmed and drained. Decisions loom large on the horizon while I barely have the courage to face today. Desperately trying to succeed in a wide spectrum of life areas, I meet with failure and grow more discouraged.

Like the girls down the hall, some days all that I have the strength to do is fall face down, oblivious to my surroundings. Yet I know that I serve a God with the most wonderful sense of humor, a God who sends me choruses of hallelujahs, even while I am wallowing in my own uncertainty and brokenness. Even when I am too exhausted to hear it, the background music to my life, a symphony of love and praise, is provided by my Lord. And even when I am too discouraged to realize what is playing, He fills my days with song.

Remind me today, Lord, that even in the midst
of my doubts and struggles, You take great delight in me.
Even when I am unable to hear the music,
You rejoice over me with singing.

Wisdom for the Week

DAY 1: PSALM 40:9-11

DAY 2: NEHEMIAH 9:9-13

DAY 3: EXODUS 18:8-11

DAY 4: JEREMIAH 31:10-14

DAY 5: PSALM 47:1-6

Some Scriptural Delights

Psalm 1:1-3

> Blessed is the man who does not walk in the counsel
> > of the wicked
> or stand in the way of sinners
> > or sit in the seat of mockers.
> But his delight is in the law of the LORD,
> > and on his law he meditates day and night.
> He is like a tree planted by streams of water,
> > which yields its fruit in season
> and whose leaf does not wither.
> > Whatever he does prospers.

Psalm 37:3-5, *KJV*

> Trust in the LORD, and do good;
> > so shalt thou dwell in the land,
> > and verily though shalt be fed.
> Delight thyself also in the LORD:
> > and he shall give thee the desires of thine heart.
> Commit thy way unto the LORD;
> > trust also in him; and he shall bring it to pass.

39

Love with Love

Letting God's Love Shine

By Annalyse Lynn Baziuk, Sonoma State University

In everything set them an example by doing what is good.
In your teaching show integrity, seriousness and soundness of speech
that cannot be condemned, so that those who oppose you may be
ashamed because they have nothing bad to say about us.

TITUS 2:7-8

Being a Christian at my school in freethinking Northern California is difficult sometimes. I work as a student assistant in an office on campus and am the only believer in the office. Consequently, I'm very shy about expressing my faith and ideals, knowing that no one would agree with me. One day, my coworkers started discussing Mel Gibson's film *The Passion of the Christ*. None of them understood the truth behind the movie, and each had her own theory about who or what God is. After much hesitation, I meekly entered the conversation and explained the movie according to the Bible.

The conversation then turned into a friendly debate—them against me. Being extremely intimidated by these ladies, by their authority and their confidence, I tried my best to explain God's version of the truth without screaming, "You're wrong!" I prayed for God's voice to be in every word I spoke, but I walked away knowing that no one really believed what I had said.

God heard those prayers, though. I returned to my job after summer vacation, and on my first day back, one of the ladies I had talked to on that day months ago told me that she had accepted Christ as her Savior over the summer. She thanked me for talking so calmly and listening so non-judgmentally in our conversation about the movie.

After thinking about the whole situation, I've realized that it wasn't my words that had left an impression with my new "sister"—it was the love with which I spoke them.

The feelings we convey with our words often overpower the meaning of the words themselves. As Christians, we are to set an example "in everything" so that people can have "nothing bad to say about us." This concept applies not only to our words but to our actions and attitudes as well. Whatever situation we're in, people notice and respond to a Christlike love. To show the love of Christ is to become transparent and let God's love shine through us. This is one of the highest goals of the Christian walk. And when we tell others about God while demonstrating God's love, He will work wonders.

Wisdom for the Week

DAY 1: HEBREWS 3:1-5

DAY 2: MATTHEW 18:1-5

DAY 3: LEVITICUS 19:18,34

DAY 4: 2 CORINTHIANS 5:14-21

DAY 5: ISAIAH 43:1-3; MATTHEW 25:34-40

Five Popular Cheap-Date Ideas

1. See a movie at a bargain theater.

2. Visit the neighborhood coffee shop.

3. Stroll through a local park.

4. Get ice-cream cones.

5. Eat at the campus cafeteria.

40

Shortcuts

Choosing to Do the Right Thing

By Karen Elledge, Azusa Pacific University

LORD, who may dwell in your sanctuary? Who may live on your holy hill? He whose walk is blameless and who does what is righteous.

PSALM 15:1-3

During my freshman year at college, I was suddenly faced with more personal choices than ever before. Suddenly I could make my own decisions, without my parents looking over my shoulder or pushing me toward the right choice.

Some of these choices were pretty straightforward and not too earth-shattering, such as deciding when to go to bed at night and what kind of vegetables to eat (or not eat!) in the cafeteria.

Many of the choices I was faced with, although seemingly trivial, were actually important ethical matters. I was tempted to sneak into the cafeteria without paying when money got tight. I was tempted to bend the rules on take-home tests, copy my friends' CDs and turn in the same essay for two different classes.

These actions seemed like easy, economical shortcuts to save a little money, time and work. After all, doesn't everyone do these things? No one really cares one way or the other, right?

No matter how I tried to justify my actions, however, I still felt guilty. I realized that yielding to such little temptations not only weakened my personal integrity but also interfered with my relationship with God. Trying to bend the rules and get away with as much as possible could not help me.

Each semester brings new temptations to cut corners, but I know God is always there to help me resist. God's way is infinitely better than my way.

Now each time I am tempted to do something I know I shouldn't, I try to ask God for the strength to do what is right.

So I strive always to keep my conscience clear before God and man.
ACTS 24:16

Wisdom for the Week

DAY 1: PROVERBS 14:5-14
DAY 2: PSALM 63
DAY 3: PROVERBS 19:1-5
DAY 4: PSALM 11:2-7
DAY 5: ACTS 5:1-5

Fool's Gold

The first of April is traditionally the day to play pranks with relative impunity. Yet it's not the only day to have some fun. Sometimes you need a little laugh to relieve the stress of the semester, so here are some ideas for harmless shenanigans:

• Stick a Post-it Note under your friend's computer mouse, covering the ball or light diode.

- Glue eggs into the carton, or swap some of the raw eggs with hard-boiled ones.

- Put the most annoying songs you can find on your roommate's iPod. Change the titles so that they're hard to find and delete.

- Decorate a shoebox or brick of foam rubber to look like a cake.

- Tell your cafeteria dinner companions what you learned in chemistry today: The lipids in Jell-O and the sodium in salt react to release energy in the form of heat. When they hold their hand over the bowl of Jell-O you've just salted, smash it down.

- Leave an official-sounding phone message for a friend from the Dean of Student Affairs.

- In your friend's word-processing program (which should have a shortcut that allows you to substitute words), set up a shortcut to change every "the" to "thermonuclear."

- Find someone to play along and announce your engagement to your friends.

—Heather Buchanan, Chapman University

41

Perfect Plans

Relying on God's Guidance

By Kim Brokate, Biola University

"For I know the plans I have for you," declares the LORD, "plans to prosper you and not to harm you, plans to give you hope and a future."
JEREMIAH 29:11

Out for a walk, my friend Anne and I were desperate to fill our empty stomachs. Famished but broke, we searched the ground for change, fantasizing about the couple pieces of sushi we could afford once we collected enough money.

After a while, we found (or scrounged from passing friends) enough money to buy the coveted sushi. With coin-filled hands, we stood on the corner across the street from the Japanese restaurant, when a man who was also waiting for the light to change turned toward us. I immediately recognized him: He had been at Our Daily Bread, a local program for the homeless and hungry. Earlier that week I had served him soup.

The man asked if we could spare any change. My friend and I exchanged glances. Without a word, Anne poured our two handfuls of change into his palms. He thanked us repeatedly and seemed so grateful that we just had to smile. My friend and I crossed the street, joyfully talking about the small, miraculous coincidence we had just experienced. We didn't know the best twist was yet to come.

On the far side of the street, we bumped into a girl we knew from school. She told us that she had just been to the restaurant that was our destination, and they were out of sushi for the day. Anne and I looked at each other and laughed.

After spending hours on our quest for sushi, we realized that God had a different purpose for us that day. We could have denied the man our handful of change and kept to *our* plan—but in the end, we wouldn't have been satisfied. Aside from missing out on sushi, we would have felt guilty for being so selfish.

God's plan is so superior to our own, we can't conceive it or predict it. We sometimes laugh and shake our heads at happenstance—without realizing that luck and chance have nothing to do with it. It was no fluke that my friend and I decided to scrounge for change that day. It was no coincidence that we found ourselves on the same corner as the man we'd met at Our Daily Bread earlier that week. It was all God. He had a plan for our day, and He has a plan for our lives. And it is a far better plan—full of twists and minor miracles—than we could ever imagine on our own.

Many are the plans in a man's heart, but it is the
LORD's purpose that prevails.
PROVERBS 19:21

Wisdom for the Week

DAY 1: PSALM 18:7-10
DAY 2: LUKE 12:16-21
DAY 3: DEUTERONOMY 24:12-15
DAY 4: PSALM 36:5-9
DAY 5: PSALM 113:5-7

Top 10 Movies Students Take to College

1. *Napoleon Dynamite*

2. *The Princess Bride*

3. *Braveheart*

4. *Dumb and Dumber*

5. *Star Wars* series

6. *How to Lose a Guy in Ten Days*

7. *Lord of the Rings* trilogy

8. *Pirates of the Caribbean* trilogy

9. *Ferris Bueller's Day Off*

10. *Indiana Jones* series

Honorable Mentions: *The Incredibles* and *Tommy Boy*

The Destructive Path

Turning Bad Choices Around

By Matthew Williams, Biola University

Enter through the narrow gate. For wide is the gate and broad is the road that leads to destruction, and many enter through it. But small is the gate and narrow the road that leads to life, and only a few find it.

MATTHEW 7:13-14

The room spun, and my temples pounded. I tried to get up off the floor, but I couldn't. My head weighed a ton, but I managed to lift it enough to survey my surroundings. The white toilet and gray tiled walls told me I was on the floor of someone's bathroom. Had I been there a few minutes or a few hours? My head really started to throb as I realized I had no idea where I was or how I got there. An empty beer can to my left jogged my memory. I was at a house party, and I was hammered. I must have gone into the bathroom to throw up and passed out on the floor instead.

I grabbed the edges of the counter and dragged myself to my feet. There I stood in front of the sink, looking at a mirror, which held the grim reflection of someone I didn't even know. "How did I get here?" I asked my reflection. I didn't mean my location; I meant my spiritual state. How did I manage to fall so far so fast?

My road down the destructive path started out looking less dangerous than it was. I was tempted by little things—having a beer with a friend or sharing a cigarette with a coworker.

From there, things snowballed uncontrollably. Having a few beers with the guys led to pounding 12-packs at parties. That, in turn, led to experimenting with marijuana and other substances. By the end of my freshman year, I was smoking weed every weekday and getting drunk every weekend—and if God hadn't gotten a hold of me, that lifestyle might have led to my early death.

The next morning as I drove home from the party, still hung over and reeking of alcohol and vomit, I decided I had to change my life. I asked God for the strength to quit drinking and smoking and for help to come back to Him.

In the next few weeks, the Lord did some amazing things in my life. He led me to an accountability group with some guys on my floor when I got back to college. He blessed me with a new group of friends who were there to build me up and encourage me. I found a fulfillment in Christ that drugs and alcohol could never give.

It is dangerous to let sin begin to creep into our hearts. The devil uses seemingly innocent things to bring us down, and we cannot let him gain a foothold in our lives.

Wisdom for the Week

DAY 1: LUKE 22:24-32
DAY 2: 2 PETER 2:4-10
DAY 3: PSALM 38:4-15
DAY 4: PSALM 41:4-9
DAY 5: 1 CORINTHIANS 6:19-20

Alcohol and the American College Student

From the Institute for Social Research at the University of Michigan:

- Forty percent of American college students are classified as heavy drinkers (having five or more drinks in a row at least once during a one-month period).

- Males use alcohol more than females.

- White students drink more frequently than Black or Hispanic students.

From the National Institute on Alcohol Abuse and Alcoholism:

- Each year, nearly 2,000 individuals under the age of 21 are killed in motor vehicle accidents that involve underage drinking.

- Alcohol consumption may permanently affect the intellectual capabilities of students' developing brains and may also increase their propensity for alcohol addiction.

- More than one million teenagers in 2002 had developed drinking behaviors so serious that they qualified for admission into alcohol treatment programs.[1]

Note

1. "High-Risk Drinking in College: What We Know and What We Need to Learn" (NIAAA College Materials: Panel Report Executive Summary 2002). *College Drinking—Changing the Culture* website, http://www.collegedrinking prevention.gov. "Statistics on Underage Drinking," *National Institute on Alcohol Abuse and Alcoholism,* http://www.niaaa.nih.gov; P. M. O'Malley and L. D. Johnston,, "Epidemiology of Alcohol and Other Drug Use Among American College Students," J Studies Alcohol Suppl. March 2002. (14):23-39, Pub-Med. National Center for Biotechnology Information homepage, http://www.ncbi.nlm.gov.

A Time of Silence

Hearing the Heart of God

By Megan Wilhelm, Spring Arbor University

But the LORD is in his holy temple; let all the earth be silent before him.
HABAKKUK 2:20

I sit at my computer keyboard a tired girl. My feet are sore, my eyes ache and my brain can't hold another fact. As I adjust to another semester here at college, my life is unbelievably hectic. Papers and tests, work and friends—my days are so busy that all the time I can spare for God is a quick prayer at the end of the day.

I want to be successful and put my all into every day, but sitting here, I feel like I can't go on. I can't go on in this crazy life that leaves me exhausted and unable to enjoy the things around me. I can't go on without spending time with God.

What I need is a time of silence—a time when I'm alert, not half asleep, a time when I can intentionally bask in the presence of my Lord. This isn't a time when I drill Him with all that is wrong in my life and all that I need. Instead, it should be a time when I relax and let Him speak to me—a time of simply listening for His voice in my life, a voice that is so often eclipsed by all life's busyness. It's a voice that can speak to my heart if I make the time and quiet my spirit.

In 1 Kings 19:11-12, the prophet Elijah is waiting for the presence of the Lord to pass by him. A great wind, an earthquake and a fire all pass by, but God is not in those elements.

The presence of God is finally found in a whisper. A whisper!

How will we ever find God in our noisy lives if we don't stop to listen for Him?

The days ahead will still be exhausting, I admit, but there is a certain joy and encouragement found in sitting at the feet of God. Our lives at college are so unbelievably busy, but we all need to spend time with God. It is in Him that we find the strength to face whatever lies ahead.

It is in silence that we hear the heart of God.

Wisdom for the Week

DAY 1: PSALM 51:6-12

DAY 2: 1 PETER 1:13-21

DAY 3: PSALM 80:1-7

DAY 4: PSALM 66:16-20

DAY 5: EPHESIANS 6:10-17

Tips for Stress Relief

- **Talk**. Sometimes a good heart-to-heart brings things into perspective and helps you clarify your problems as you put them into words. Don't whine; just be honest and accurate. Be ready to listen, too!

- **Laugh**. In some cases, laughter really *is* the best medicine. Rent a Marx Brothers movie, play a prank on a friend or sit next to that guy who tells great stories when you go to the cafeteria. Nothing clears your head like a good, hard laugh.

- **Move**. We get so busy with all our commitments, it's easy to cut out exercise—but there are few better ways to blow off steam and clear your mind than a few minutes on the treadmill or in a pickup game of basketball. Get those endorphins flowing.

- **Simplify**. A lot of our stress comes from being over-committed or from wanting more than we really need. Cut through the clutter. Consider getting rid of those activities, possessions and ambitions that keep you too busy.

- **Waste some time with God**. Not all your time with God has to be Bible study and fervent prayer. Waste some time with Him. You can spare a half hour! Find a nice lawn and lie on your back looking up at the clouds He has made. Skip some stones. Collect some fallen leaves. Sit with your back against a tree and listen to some favorite music.

When It Is Okay to Trust

Confiding in the Father

By Amber Kay Friudenberg, University of Texas at Austin

Do you not know? Have you not heard? The LORD is the everlasting
God, the Creator of the ends of the earth. He will not grow tired or
weary, and his understanding no one can fathom.
ISAIAH 40:28

I think we college students sometimes get very caught up in . . . well, college; and we forget that we do not have to understand God—we just have to trust Him.

In July 2004, I found out my dad had cancer. Unfortunately, I was away from home for the summer, and I was unable to be with him as much as I would have liked. I was able to spend a month at home in August, but then I was quickly swept back to busy days on campus.

Three months later, my father died. He had gone from a healthy, 57-year-old man—who had planned to run in the Senior Olympics—to a frail, thin man who could no longer climb the front-porch steps.

When I got the news of his death, I wondered how I could ever make it without my dad. Life worried me; college scared me; I couldn't imagine ever getting through a week without weeping over so great a loss in my life. I was angry, incensed that my wonderful friend and father had been taken. No one I had ever known was like my dad.

Slowly I began to realize that I may never know why my wonderful father was taken—but God, in His infinite power, understands all things. God looks at me with love, and He hurts when I hurt. Isaiah says that God is distressed when His people are distressed, and Romans 8:28 says, "In all things God works for the good of those who love him."

The world is a confusing, disturbing, strange place at times, but God holds our hands. He has promised never to leave us or forsake us. And on those days when we need to crawl up in our Dad's lap, He always has the time to let us have a good cry.

Life, when we look through the eyes of our Savior, is truly magnificent. Like Christ, we will endure pain, but through it we will grow and change and become more Christlike.

We don't have to micromanage our lives, because our *Abba*—our Daddy—is big enough to love us, protect us, guide us and, ultimately, save us from all things—including our own worst fears.

Wisdom for the Week

DAY 1: ISAIAH 63:7-9
DAY 2: ISAIAH 41:13-14
DAY 3: PSALM 59:16-17
DAY 4: DEUTERONOMY 31:1-6
DAY 5: PSALM 66:16-20

Sources of Stress and Anxiety

University life brings newfound independence—no more asking for parental permission. However, that freedom brings its own pressures. Campus life is not utopia. Students report that the following issues cause them worry and stress:

- Money matters—financing tuition, taking on student loans, graduating with debt

- Dating relationships or the lack thereof

- Academic pressures—maintaining academic scholarships, taking exams, writing essays, completing ongoing assignments

- Roommate conflicts

- The future—choosing a major, a career, a mate; finding one's place in the world

- Computer equipment problems—crashed hard drives, printer trouble, lost files

- Conflicts with parents—fulfilling parental expectations for success, getting along as adults

- Procrastination

- Lack of sleep

- Dealing with campus bureaucracies—financial aid offices, registration nightmares

- Illness

- Car trouble—mechanical breakdowns, finding a parking space, not having a vehicle

He Lives

Believing in What Comes After

By Kristen Orem, Biola University

*Jesus said to her, "I am the resurrection and the life;
he who believes in Me will live even if he dies."*
JOHN 11:25, *NASB*

Easter was my grandpa's favorite holiday. He and my grand-mother lived next door to us, so we were very close. After church on Easter Sunday, the two of them would come over to our house for Easter lunch, which we'd eat at tables in front of our houses; and then all my cousins and I would search for Easter eggs through our connected gardens.

That was the first thing I loved about Easter: all those brightly colored plastic eggs hidden under bushes, slipped into planters or nestled between the flowers in Grandpa's corner garden. Grandpa would follow us as we searched, sometimes giving us hints or pretending to try to steal the candy from our baskets.

When all the eggs had been found, I'd climb up in his lap. "*Perlita*," he'd say to me, "let's see what you found." And I'd crack open the plastic eggs and share my chocolate with him.

The first Easter after Grandpa's death was difficult for us all. He passed away when I was just five years old, and even though I did not understand many things about his death, I did know he was up in heaven. That year we went through our usual Easter traditions: the meal after church and the hunt for eggs—but there was no Grandpa to share my candy with.

That afternoon my mother and my grandma were sitting at one of the outdoor tables where we'd gathered for our Easter lunch when they looked and saw me in my little frilly dress, standing by myself in the driveway. I was jumping up and throwing pieces of my chocolate straight up in the air. When they fell to the ground, I'd pick them up and throw them again.

The two of them watched me a while, and then my mom called out to me, "What on earth are you doing, sweetie?"

I looked up at them, red faced with exertion. "I'm giving Grandpa his chocolate," I said. I was sure he was in heaven. I knew he was literally there, even though I couldn't see him.

Seventeen years later, I still cling to my belief in the resurrection. Christ literally died on the cross and He literally came back to life on Easter morning. The story of the resurrection isn't *just* a story; it's something that really happened.

And because of that, I know Grandpa lives.

Wisdom for the Week

DAY 1: MARK 15:25-38
DAY 2: MATTHEW 27:57-66
DAY 3: LUKE 23:44-56
DAY 4: MATTHEW 28:1-10
DAY 5: LUKE 24:1-12

An American Easter Tradition

The Monday after Easter, the White House hosts an Easter Egg Roll. Each year as many as 17,000 people enter the South Lawn where children use long-handled spoons to roll colored eggs (and sometimes themselves) down the grassy slope. They also search for hidden eggs and listen to stories read by authors and political figures.

The tradition began on the grounds of the Capitol building. As early as 1872, newspaper coverage related stories of children in Washington rolling eggs across the Capitol lawn. The activity proved too much for the grass, however, so in 1876 Congress passed a Turf Protection Law that prohibited children from engaging in any more egg rolls. Then in 1878, President Rutherford B. Hayes saved the event by inviting the children to have their fun on the White House lawn instead.

The First Family often presides over the egg-rolling festivities, which may include a variety of activities. More than 7,000 real eggs are provided for the roll, roughly 3,000 dyed for the Egg Hunt and 4,000 boiled for decorating. In addition, children receive a decorated wooden egg to commemorate the day.

The National Park Service distributes free tickets beginning a couple of days before the event. Every attendee must have a ticket, and for adults to gain admittance, a child seven years or under must attend with them.

The egg has long been a symbol of Easter, and rolling the egg represents the stone that was rolled from the Savior's tomb.

Thief

Taking Peace over Fear

By Sara Van Valkenburg, Biola University

Surely God is my help: the Lord is the one who sustains me.
PSALM 54:4

My dorm was quiet; my roommate had just gone to bed, and I was writing a paper. A few minutes after one A.M., one of my friends stopped by to talk. We were sitting there chatting when I heard a noise at the window. We both turned and saw a strange man standing outside in the shadows.

To my utter shock, he reached in the window, grabbed my roommate's laptop and disappeared into the night. I screamed, and our room soon filled with girls from my hall. I hadn't been hurt, but in a matter of seconds my perception of a secure life in a safe world were altered forever.

Over the next weeks, my fear did not go away. I would be sitting in class when the thief's image would intrude my thoughts. A friend's squeal of laughter would make my heart pound. I would even jump when I saw my roommate's reflection in the mirror. I imagined the prowler lurked around every corner.

My fear became even more intense when campus security officers showed me pictures and asked me if I could identify any of them as the man who stole the computer. Were there really so many bad people out there?

It took me a long time to get over the anxiety that one thief introduced to my life that night, but the truth eventually dawned on me: Peace and fear could not reside in my heart at the same time. And God wanted me to have peace.

Though I felt alone, God helped me overcome my fear. He is the place of safety and sanctuary, in spite of any struggles and dangers we face.

As a college student, being off on your own for the first time can introduce all kinds of new worries: *Will I get along with my roommate? Will I pass my classes? Will I be homesick?* You can trust God's peace through the anxiety and difficulties.

Wisdom for the Week

DAY 1: PROVERBS 29:11-27
DAY 2: JOHN 14:23-27
DAY 3: PSALM 4
DAY 4: LAMENTATIONS 3:21-32
DAY 5: NUMBERS 14:1-9

Safety Tips

It is easy to become complacent after a few peaceful weeks or months of living in your campus dorm or apartment. However, no campus is a crime-free zone, so keep these guidelines in mind:

Housing

- Keep track of keys. Never loan keys to others. Report lost or stolen keys immediately.
- Don't leave doors unlocked or propped open.

- Don't admit unknown persons into dormitories or other campus housing (even if they look harmless).
- Keep doors and accessible windows locked at all times.

Possessions

- Don't leave laptop computers, backpacks or other personal items unattended in libraries, study rooms, dining halls, bookstores or other public or private areas.
- Keep an inventory of the personal articles in your living quarters. Mark expensive items for identification in case they are lost or stolen.
- Store cash, credit cards, checkbooks and other important documents out of sight in a secure area.

Walking

- Travel in groups. Always avoid secluded areas.
- Request a campus escort when walking to remote parking areas or when leaving campus in the dark.
- Don't let cell-phone conversations distract you. Be aware of your surroundings.
- Trust your instincts. Report any suspicious or strange behavior or activity.

Vehicles

- Lock bicycles and cars at all times.
- Store valuables out of sight or in the trunk of your car.
- Never sleep, eat or study in your car. (Carjackers prey on drivers who sit unaware in their vehicles, even in daylight or in well-lighted areas.)
- Always check the backseat of your car before you open the door.

Seasons

Learning Patience as Life Unfolds

By Anne Davis, University of Minnesota, Twin Cities

There is a time for everything, and a season for every activity under heaven.
ECCLESIASTES 3:1

In *The Empire Strikes Back*, Jedi master Yoda is reluctant to allow the young apprentice Luke Skywalker to begin his Jedi training. "This one a long time have I watched," Yoda says. "All his life has he looked away . . . to the future, to the horizon. Never his mind on where he was [or] what he was doing."

I am so blind to the present. I spend most of my time being nostalgic about the past or daydreaming about the future. *If only I could be done with this semester, be back on the mountaintop, be married right now, be _____ (fill in the blank)!*

One day the Lord asked me why I had not opened my eyes to the beauty and meaning of where He has placed me now. I was willing the time to go by more quickly or more slowly, and I realized that these seasons are not meant to be rushed or extended. Through each period of my life, God has presented me with unique blessings and challenges necessary for the good work that He is doing in me (see Philippians 1:6). It is a lesson that is relevant for every moment of my life.

I've often tried to grab at good things that the Lord has withheld. I've realized that these things are not necessarily bad—

but maybe they are meant for another season of my life. He has shown me that He desires to give me His best, if only I am patient and wait for Him. I remember His promise:

> On this mountain, the Lord Almighty will prepare a feast of rich food for all peoples, a banquet of aged wine—the best of meats and the finest of wines (Isaiah 25:6).

Do we trust God with our lives? So often we sit down and write out our lives according to our timing and our plan. But living our lives this way will never come close to the greatness He has in store for us (see 1 Corinthians 2:9). So let us lay down our pens and allow our loving Father to unfold His beautiful plan for our lives in His own timing.

He has made everything beautiful in its time.
ECCLESIASTES 3:11

Wisdom for the Week

DAY 1: ECCLESIASTES 3:1-11
DAY 2: JOHN 17:1-12
DAY 3: PROVERBS 20:24-30
DAY 4: 1 CORINTHIANS 1:20-25
DAY 5: PSALM 27:7-14

Movie Wisdom

- "There's no place like home."—*The Wizard of Oz* (1939)

- "After all . . . tomorrow is another day."—*Gone with the Wind* (1939)

- "Faith is believing when common sense tells you not to."—*Miracle on 34th Street* (1947)

- "His strength will never die, Saul. Men will tell his story for a thousand years."—*Samson and Delilah* (1949)

- "After all that men could do had failed, the Martians were destroyed and humanity was saved by the littlest things which God, in His wisdom, had put upon this Earth."—*War of the Worlds* (1953)

- "Well, nobody's perfect."—*Some Like It Hot* (1959)

- "All I wanna do is go the distance."—*Rocky* (1976)

- "Roads? Where we're going, we don't need roads." —*Back to the Future* (1985)

- "I came here tonight because when you realize you want to spend the rest of your life with somebody, you want the rest of your life to start as soon as possible."—*When Harry Met Sally* (1989)

- "Mama always said, 'Life was like a box of chocolates. You never know what you're gonna get.'"—*Forrest Gump* (1994)

- "Vengeance is a lazy form of grief."—*The Interpreter* (2005)

48

Flight

Soaring with Confidence

By Mary Eriksson, Point Loma Nazarene University

*The LORD gives strength to his people; the LORD blesses
his people with peace.*

PSALM 29:11

Light and hazy, the heat of the noon-day sun filters through the
eucalyptus trees and lingers in the air, like the pungent scent of
the silver leaves above me. I have so little time left here; graduation is just two months away. How many more chances will I
have to sit and learn on the steps of the Greek Theater? How
many more opportunities to discuss feminist literary theory while
sitting in the sun, squinting out at the ocean that looks hazy
now, fading off into the sky and the horizon? A gull silently
swoops and glides, slicing the sea smoothly from the sky.

It's a strange feeling: I love this place, but I am ready to
move on. I am not afraid that I won't find this feeling again—
that I won't ever capture the peace I feel and the beauty I see, or
find friends who share my intellectual interests. As I sit here in
this familiar place, it is both reassuring and unnerving to know
that it's not this university that gives me peace; no place or
community can.

The idea of losing this sense of security could leave me
floating, feeling about as sure of my existence as that hazy

ocean horizon. But thank You, Father, that I can sit here, grounded by Your love and grace and in the knowledge that no matter where I go from here, I am in Christ and You are in me. This is my identity. With this knowledge, my spirit soars like that gull, free and boundless, reveling in the spring breeze and freedom of flight. In two months I will take flight myself, and the horizon will become clearer than I see now with my squinty eyes. I am ready.

Thank You, Lord, for this world and for holding me in Your palm as I sit and gaze at that vast blue ocean. I know You are Lord over all, and that "the voice of the LORD is over the waters, the God of glory thunders, the LORD is over many waters. The voice of the LORD is powerful; the voice of the LORD is majestic" (Psalm 29:3-4, *NASB*).

I know You are the God of the ocean—and of all that is mysterious and unknown. You are with me, and You hold my life in Your hands. I am confident of this, because "the LORD sat as King at the flood; yes, the LORD sits as King forever. The LORD will give strength to His people; the LORD will bless His people with peace" (Psalm 29:10-11, *NASB*).

Wisdom for the Week

DAY 1: PSALM 10:14-18
DAY 2: ACTS 11:19-25
DAY 3: PSALM 23
DAY 4: PSALM 32:6-11
DAY 5: ISAIAH 49:8-13

Pomp and Circumstance

Here are a few facts about the graduation ceremony, which has its roots in medieval times, that might help you make sense of it:

The Robe
Typically there are three kinds, each of which indicates the level of the wearer's degree: (1) the bachelor's robe, a plain robe without adornment and with long, bell-shaped sleeves (2) the master's robe, which has dangling oblong sleeves closed at the ends; (3) the doctorate's robes, with three velvet stripes on each sleeve.

The Mortarboard
Most of the people you see at graduation wear mortarboards. (Some who hold doctorates may wear a pillowy kind of four-, six- or eight-cornered hat called a tam.) When the bachelor's degree is conferred, the wearer moves the tassel on the mortarboard from the left to the right.

The Hood
Hoods vary in length, depending on the wearer's degree (longer hood for higher degree). The hood hangs around the wearer's neck and dangles down the back. The colors of the hood's satin lining indicate the school where the degree was awarded, while the color of the velvet trim indicates the field of study.

The Music
That song you keep hearing as everyone marches in is Edward Elgar's "Pomp and Circumstance." It was first played at a graduation ceremony at Yale University in 1905, when Elgar himself was awarded an honorary doctorate of music. Thereafter it was adopted by a number of other prestigious American universities and is now standard fare for graduations across the U.S.

49

My Greatest Fear

Losing Faith, Finding Faith

By Alicia Shocki, Montreat College

See to it, brothers, that none of you has a sinful, unbelieving heart
that turns away from the living God.

HEBREWS 3:12

Exactly two years ago, I lost my faith in the Lord.

I spent my whole life in a Christian home. In fact, I am a PK (which, if you don't know, stands for "pastor's kid"). I was only three years old when I first gave my life to Christ, and my life after that revolved around church. Without ever questioning it, I believed that Jesus was my one and only Savior—that is what I had always been taught. Sometimes church was fun—we had laser tag and all-night lock-ins—but otherwise it was an obligation I had to fulfill. My parents made me go. It was more about my social life than my spiritual life.

When I got a bit older, I came to the conclusion that my relationship with Christ had to be more than something I was taught at church. I realized that I had to develop a relationship with God just like I would with any of my friends or family. I had to spend time with Him, reading His Word and talking with Him. I had to decide if I wanted to continue on a path based on my faith in Christ. I decided—on my own—that I wanted to pursue a relationship and make the Lord my priority.

I struggled with spending time with the Lord daily. I struggled with everything a normal teenager would grapple with. But I kept telling myself I was committed to God. No matter how much I screwed up, I was His. He was my purpose, and I knew that I had forgiveness and peace in Him. Around that time, someone asked me what my greatest fear was. I told him the truth: losing my faith.

And then it happened. I surrendered the struggle. I lost my faith. For four months, I pushed God away. I dug a hole and hid in it. I let the influences of the world affect my thinking. I came to the conclusion that God existed, but He had no place in my life. Like Hebrews 3:12 warns, I had "a sinful, unbelieving heart," and I turned away. My biggest fear had come true, and I did not even care.

But even though I had given up on God, He hadn't give up on me. He was with me every doubting step, carrying me when the world seemed like it might crash in on me. Four months after I lost my faith, God brought me back to Him. He dragged me out of the hole I had been hiding in.

I realized there was nothing I could do to develop a relationship with Christ. He was the One who opened the door and allowed me to know Him and be loved by Him. My reaching up to Him meant nothing compared to His reaching down to me.

Wisdom for the Week

DAY 1: MATTHEW 14:22-33

DAY 2: JOHN 20:9-29

DAY 3: MATTHEW 6:25-33

DAY 4: PSALM 146:1-10

DAY 5: LUKE 7:1-10

Faith

When those feelings of doubt and discouragement crowd your brain and cloud your peace, take some time to contemplate these scriptural truths:

- The fundamental fact of existence is that this trust in God, this faith, is the firm foundation under everything that makes life worth living. It's our handle on what we can't see (Hebrews 11:1, *THE MESSAGE*).

- Be prepared. You're up against far more than you can handle on your own. Take all the help you can get, every weapon God has issued, so that when it's all over but the shouting you'll still be on your feet (Ephesians 6:13, *THE MESSAGE*).

- By entering through faith into what God has always wanted to do for us—set us right with him, make us fit for him—we have it all together with God because of our Master Jesus. And that's not all: We throw open our doors to God and discover at the same moment that he has already thrown open his door to us (Romans 5:1-2, *THE MESSAGE*).

- There's more to come: We continue to shout our praise even when we're hemmed in with troubles, because we know how troubles can develop passionate patience in us, and how that patience in turn forges the tempered steel of virtue, keeping us alert for whatever God will do next (Romans 5:1-4, *THE MESSAGE*).

50

Would You Like Fries with That?

Working for the Lord

By Ryan Simmons, Cedarville University

> *Many are the plans in a man's heart,*
> *but it is the LORD's purpose that prevails.*
> PROVERBS 19:21

I remember as a kid—in elementary school, junior high and even in high school—looking forward to the summer as one long Saturday morning. It was the end of another school year and a time of cartoon-watching, sunny weather, swimming, water fights and family road trips. The days were long and the nights were warm. Best of all, summer was a time of freedom, when only bedtime limited what I could and couldn't do in any given day.

But alas, such days are gone. As I near the end of another semester in my college career, I no longer face such open-ended freedom. I face the threat of something worse: the summer job search. Now I must approach life as an adult and face the school bills that pile up on my already large mountain of car payments, phone bills and girlfriend expenses. I have discovered, sadly, that there are no orchards of vibrant-green money trees blossoming with fresh dollar bills.

I've also found that summer employment is not about being selective. I would like to think of myself as an educated, mature university student on the brink of greatness—but the rest of the world doesn't quite see me that way. In the end, if I want to get a job and make a little money for school, I've got to foster the sort of humility that will say, "Yes, I will make a hamburger with cheese and extra pickles," or "Yes, I will work on this mindless assembly line for the next 12 hours," or even "Yes, ma'am, will that be paper or plastic?"

Ultimately, it doesn't matter if a summer job forces me to wear a funny hat, paste a smile on my face or callous my hands in long hours of dirty work. Ultimately, I am doing what God wants me to do and doing it where He wants me to do it. This is the job He had planned for me from the beginning of time, and I will do it to His glory—even if it means deep-frying the best fries in town.

As a wise man once said, "A man who works to the glory of God will never have a mundane job."

Wisdom for the Week

DAY 1: ECCLESIASTES 5:15-20

DAY 2: DEUTERONOMY 2:1-7

DAY 3: PROVERBS 10:1-5

DAY 4: PROVERBS 30:5-8

DAY 5: 2 THESSALONIANS 3:6-10

The Art of the Job Interview

If you're out applying for a summer job, you're probably in for the most nerve-wracking part of getting hired: the interview. Here are a few tips that might help you look poised and professional when the questions start flying:

- **Do your homework.** Almost every outfit you'll ever interview with has got something on the Web about them. Look it over.

- **Look confident.** Shake hands. Make eye contact. Smile. Show good manners. Sure, interviews are scary, but if you look composed you'll make a better impression.

- **Dress well.** As a general rule, dress a little better than the job you're applying for requires—dress nicely, but don't overdo it (a suit might be a little much for that lifeguard interview).

- **Talk to everyone.** If there are two or three people around the table, talk to them all and look at them all when your give your answers. Don't address all your comments to the person you think is the boss (you might be wrong). Including everyone makes you look like a team player.

- **Ask questions.** Sure, you'll mostly be giving answers, but asking questions shows that you're really interested in this place and what they do.

- **Follow up.** A simple email or note thanking your interviewer will highlight your interest in the job and make you look persistent and professional—and it will also remind them who you are.

51

Lessons from My Dad

Living with Open Hands

By Katie Putnam, University of Georgia

The LORD gave and the LORD has taken away;
may the name of the LORD be praised.

JOB 1:21

I can remember that every night when I was a little girl my dad would come and tuck me into bed. During those sweet times, we would talk about life. One night, I was particularly distraught. My best friend and I had had a fight, and we weren't talking to each other. I remember telling my dad that I was scared we weren't going to be best friends anymore and that I didn't want anybody else for a best friend.

My dad took my fist and said something I will never forget. He uncurled my fingers and said, "We as God's children have to hold everything with an open hand."

He then curled my fingers closed again and continued. "If we hold on to everything we have with a closed fist, when God decides that He wants to take something, He has to break our fingers to get to it."

Slowly, he pulled back my unresisting fingers one by one. "If God has to break your fingers, it will hurt a lot worse than if you just allowed Him to take what He wanted in the first place. Plus," he said as he held my open hand, "if we hold everything with an open hand, God can give us new things as well."

The God who created the oceans and formed the mountains with His hands will not be deterred from His plan by our human fingers—yet we often think that if we hold on to something hard enough, God will not be able to take it from us.

We need to understand deeply in our hearts that God does not need our permission to do anything. But we also need to know and truly believe that He doesn't take things from us to make us miserable. God knows what will make us happy much better than we do. We are better off giving everything to Him from the start.

Praise His name while you hold everything with an open hand, and watch as He strengthens your faith in Him.

Wisdom for the Week

DAY 1: PSALM 33:6-11

DAY 2: ISAIAH 40:21-26

DAY 3: MARK 12:30-33

DAY 4: 1 KINGS 2:1-4

DAY 5: JOHN 10:27-30

Father's Day

Everyone knows to send flowers on Mother's Day and to take Mom out to lunch after church—but what about Father's Day? Is it really all about a burnt-toast breakfast in bed and a tie? Here are a few ways you can remind Dad how much you love him:

- **What's Dad's passion?** Remember that thing he always wanted you to do with him when you were little? Whatever it is—playing a round of golf or watching a baseball game—take an afternoon off and do it with him.

- **Get him a gift card.** Get it from a place he likes—Starbucks or the sporting goods store or the men's-wear shop. He can even buy himself a tie if he wants to.

- **Make him something.** It's true: Dads are pushovers for anything you create yourself. Trust us, somewhere there's a drawer full of those birthday cards and plastic lanyards you kept making him in grade school.

- **What about flowers and lunch?** Dads like that stuff, too.

52

Coming Home to Christ

Taking Refuge in Transition

By Cate McCrory, Seattle Pacific University

God is our refuge and strength, an ever-present help in trouble.
Therefore we will not fear, though the earth give way.
PSALM 46:1-2

In my junior year of high school, my parents moved our family across the country from Washington, DC, to Southern California. Needless to say, landing in a new high school was rough, but because my roots hadn't grown very deep, going away to college two years later was fairly easy.

I was thrilled to head off to Seattle for my freshman year, and I came to find that college life was everything I'd hoped it would be: I made great friends, loved my classes and thrived in my new independence.

But coming home after my freshman year was another story.

I knew I was going to miss my new circle of friends and the academic environment I had come to love, but when I returned home, I found the transition even rougher than I'd imagined. For one thing, my room had more or less become one of those storage lockers people rent when their garages overflow. It was crowded with all the furniture my family had inherited from a recently passed grandparent. To top it off, my 24-year-old brother had moved back home, and my closet was stuffed with his junk. My room now held two dressers and teetering stacks of storage boxes. I didn't expect my family to preserve my room as a shrine while I was away, but I didn't think it would become a cargo hold, either.

As for my friendships in California, well, none of them seemed to compare with the new relationships I enjoyed at college. There were awkward pauses in the conversations I had with my pre-college friends, and I felt as if I had changed so much while everyone at home had stayed the same.

Home did not feel like home anymore—but college didn't feel like home, either. While I loved every minute of school, there was something rootless about living in a dorm room and knowing I'd be moving on in a few years, just like all the other students who had lived there before me. I felt in-between and unsettled.

The only thing that settled my heart was my relationship with God. Knowing that He is with me wherever I am—and will be for the rest of my life, wherever it takes me—gives me peace and comfort. I will always be at home with Him as my Savior.

Psalm 46 says that God is our refuge. He is our safe shelter, our protective home. We are rooted in Him. I give thanks that I am always at home with Christ.

Wisdom for the Week

DAY 1: LUKE 9:57-62

DAY 2: MATTHEW 8:19-27

DAY 3: PSALM 138:4-8

DAY 4: JOHN 16:25-33

DAY 5: 2 TIMOTHY 2:19-26

You Can't Go Home Again

I had spent months living a fiercely independent life in college and wasn't ready to be back under my mom's authority. I love my mom, but the thought of being mothered was overwhelming. Dealing with this transition can be difficult for many college students who spend most of the year away from home. Here are a couple of ideas that might ease the tension of that first homecoming.

First, recognize your parents will have expectations. My homecoming was nothing like my mom expected. She thought we would catch up—that I would tell her all about my classes, crushes, late nights and long days—but I was aloof. When we did talk, she thought I snapped at her or belittled her with my tone. This caused a tension between us, but we were able to work though it when I made the effort to understand my mom's expectations.

Second, help your parents notice your maturity. Mom did not seem to realize that I had matured during those months I spent in the dorms. I was determined to demonstrate this maturity to her. I worked on speaking patiently and with love, respected her by telling her I would be home around 11 P.M. on my way out the door, and took my little sister to her friends' birthday parties. Soon, Mom recognized my growth, and another source of tension dissipated.

Looking back, there was no reason for me to be so defensive. It ended up being a perfect break. I ate well, recuperated and had some great talks with my mom. Since then, I've come to understand my mom's confusion and disappointment, and I admire how she dealt with those emotions.

—Chelsey Merlo, Biola University

53

Seeing Jesus

Serving Others to Serve Christ

By Kobi Johnson, Abilene Christian University

*Is not this the kind of fasting I have chosen: to loose the chains
of injustice and untie the cords of the yoke, to set the
oppressed free and break every yoke?*

ISAIAH 58:6

Four weeks had gone by fast. It seemed like only a few days ago my friend and I had arrived in Thailand, ready to provide child care for missionaries at the annual Asian Mission Forum held at Kaew Yai Mountain Resort. Now, drained by long stretches of time supervising missionary children, we stood in line, sleepily dragging our bags with us, dreaming of the chance to sleep on the flight home.

A young woman wearing a T-shirt from an American university stood in front of us; she turned and said, "How long have you been here?" We started out of our zombie-like states and told her we had been there four weeks, caring for missionary children at a resort. When we asked her about her trip, she told us she'd spent the whole summer in Bangkok volunteering at an AIDS orphanage—she was majoring in nursing at her school and was grateful for the opportunity.

The kids she worked with were incredible, she said. Then she began telling us about their physical and emotional needs, which ran rampant—as the children themselves often did—in the streets of Bangkok.

I couldn't help but think of the mission trips I had previously taken to Thailand. I had seen countless children like the kids this woman described, but I had never offered my hand in love or service to any of them. True, I had prayed and fasted. I had spent a lot of time on my knees and several days in half or full fasts. But my hands never left the posture of prayer; I had never offered them to any of these children in love or service.

Standing in that airport line, I thought of Mother Teresa, who once said, "I see Jesus in every human being. I say to myself, this is hungry Jesus, I must feed him. This is sick Jesus. This one has leprosy or gangrene; I must wash him and tend to him. I serve because I love Jesus."

I turned to the Mother Teresa-like eyes of the woman in front of me, and my heart ached to love and serve Jesus. In the middle of the airport, I realized Jesus was all around me, in the form of children selling flowers, monks walking meekly by, fruit-selling venders and waiting taxi drivers. I suddenly saw Jesus asking for a few *baht*, searching for a smile, aching for love, hoping for the touch of a hand. And suddenly I wished I had more time to serve in Thailand.

Wisdom for the Week

DAY 1: JAMES 2:14-26

DAY 2: DEUTERONOMY 15:7-11

DAY 3: 1 JOHN 3:16-24

DAY 4: MATTHEW 26:6-13

DAY 5: MARK 16:14-20

Fourth of July Tidbits

Birthdays
- Nathaniel Hawthorne, American author (1804)
- Stephen Foster, American composer (1826)
- Calvin Coolidge, thirtieth United States president (1872)
- Ann Landers and Abigail Van Buren (Dear Abby), advice columnist twins (1918)
- Neil Simon, American playwright (1927)
- Rube Goldberg, Pulitzer Prize-winning cartoonist (1883)
- George Steinbrenner, Yankees owner (1930)

Deaths
- John Adams, second United States president (1826)
- Thomas Jefferson, third United States president (1826)
- James Monroe, fifth United States president (1831)

Lifespans
According to Ellsworth Huntington in *Seasons of Birth,* people born in July and August do not live as long as those born in February or March.[1]

Note

1. Ellsworth Huntington, cited in Gabriele Doblhammer, *The Late Life Legacy of Very Early Life (Demographic Research Monographs)* (Berlin, Germany: Springer-Verlag Publishers, 2004), p. 19.

54

Corn Dogs and Commission

Bringing God's Love to the Lonely

By Trevor Nagle, Biola University

Therefore go and make disciples of all nations, baptizing them in the name of the Father and of the Son and of the Holy Spirit, and teaching them to obey everything I have commanded you.

MATTHEW 28:19-20

"I know how it feels to be absolutely worthless," Jeff said. He stared at his paper plate, empty except for two corn dog sticks and a ketchup stain. He'd just told me he was working a new job, attending college and saving money for his next semester.

"Why do you feel worthless?" I asked. I probably could have answered the question myself. Jeff was 25, lived with his mom, was struggling through college and was working for minimum wage. He was overweight and shy. He had dreams of studying geology but wasn't doing well in basic science courses. Today he was alone at the mall with two corn dogs as company, and this was the best day he'd had in weeks.

He paused, and I wondered if I had offended him.

"You don't need to answer," I said. "I didn't mean to . . . I'm sorry."

"I don't know," he said. He picked up one of the sticks and drew a design in the ketchup. "I just feel like I am a drain on whoever I'm with. I feel worthless."

My conversation with Jeff was different from what I had expected from my first day of field ministry—a requirement for an evangelism course. The class was supposed to be easy. I figured we'd study the Great Commission, look at the life of Paul and maybe read a biography of Billy Graham. I never imagined I would end up in a mall food court, searching for an opportunity to share Christ with strangers. It was awkward and uncomfortable. I just wanted to get it over with.

Jeff was the third person I approached. I told him I was taking a course in religion, and we were supposed to ask people what they thought about life, people and God. Jeff opened up about his deep loneliness and lack of self-worth. As he shared, I saw how much he needed Christ's healing.

When he finished, I asked him if I could share something. I told him that he was not worthless, that he was in fact greatly loved by God. I told him how we are separated from a loving God because of our sins, but Christ was able to pay our penalty on the cross. As I spoke, I saw the expression on Jeff's face soften, as if, little by little, he was coming to grips with the fact that he was loved. A few minutes later, Jeff made the decision to trust Christ with his life.

Suddenly the time at the mall was no longer about me—my fear, my embarrassment, my frustrations with this assignment— it was about Jesus healing a broken life. Christ died to bring healing to our broken souls. He came to Earth to heal some people of their physical pain, to heal others of emotional pain and to offer everyone the promise of spiritual healing. Jeff's step in the mall may have been a small one, but I believe that the God who loves him enough to die for him had already begun to heal his broken life.

Wisdom for the Week

DAY 1: MARK 1:14-20

DAY 2: ACTS 8:26-39

DAY 3: 2 TIMOTHY 2:1-10

DAY 4: HEBREWS 12:1-3

DAY 5: COLOSSIANS 1:1-6

Wisdom of the Founding Fathers

Here are some thoughts from a few of our Founding Fathers:

- "What you would seem to be, be really." (Benjamin Franklin)

- "Never rise to speak till you have something to say; and when you have said it, cease." (John Witherspoon)

- "A chip on the shoulder is too heavy a piece of baggage to carry through life." (John Hancock)

- "Honesty is the first chapter in the book of wisdom." (Thomas Jefferson)

- "Our contest is not only whether we ourselves shall be free, but whether there shall be left to mankind an asylum on earth for civil and religious liberty." (Samuel Adams)

- "I always consider the settlement of America with reverence and wonder, as the opening of a grand scene and design in providence, for the illumination of the ignorant and the emancipation of the slavish part of mankind all over the earth." (John Adams)

- "Never read a book through merely because you have begun it." (John Witherspoon)

55

Shattered Pieces

Struggling with Sexual Temptation

By Heather A. Nelson [University Name Withheld]

For I will forgive their wickedness and will remember their sins no more.
HEBREWS 8:12

Growing up in a Christian home, I knew sex outside marriage was wrong. As a teenager, I attended True Love Waits conferences, led Bible studies where I encouraged young girls to remain abstinent, and faithfully wore a purity ring. A naïve and self-conscious freshman at a Christian university, I became involved with a guy I thought loved me, but it turned out he had other ideas. As our involvement progressed—from kissing, to touching, to fondling—I lost my grip on my decisions.

One night, David (not his real name) asked me to satisfy him orally. Ignoring my conscience, I did what he wanted, and almost immediately felt my life shatter. I tried to hide my brokenness—fake smiles on Sunday, hellos to friends and "I'm doing well" at work. Hiding my pain didn't help when David asked for more later on. Though I was able to say no to intercourse that night, I knew the next time would be different. I didn't *want* to say no, and that realization frightened me to my core.

Scared, confused and distraught, I pounded on my resident director's door at one o'clock in the morning. My body shaking, face streaked with tears, I explained to her the trouble I had gotten myself into. She sat with me, praying and comforting me, which eventually calmed my frightened spirit.

The process of healing and deciding to walk down the right path was difficult and continues to be a struggle, but I have taken some important steps toward mending my life's broken pieces. First, confiding in my friends was a starting point to making right choices. Being honest with trustworthy companions provided comfort, perspective and encouragement. The truth from my accountability partners helps me to make better decisions.

Second, I allowed God to forgive me and finally learned to forgive myself. The latter was the most difficult step. I was the only person I could blame for my actions. Depressing thoughts quickly overcame me, spiraling me down into a lonely place of self-hatred and depression. I had to remember that Jesus died for a reason—He didn't want me denying the forgiveness He'd already granted me.

It's easy to forget God's grace in the midst of sin. Sexual temptation is a common struggle—and not only for men, as we sometimes like to pretend. Both men and women struggle with masturbation, oral sex and intercourse. If you're struggling with sexual temptation, seek help from your close friends. If you're recovering from wrong choices, remember Who is on your side. Jesus Christ is the ultimate comforter and encourager—the only One who can mend our shattered pieces.

Wisdom for the Week

DAY 1: LUKE 15:3-10

DAY 2: JONAH 2:7-9

DAY 3: 2 SAMUEL 22:25-33

DAY 4: PROVERBS 24:1-6

DAY 5: PSALM 62:1-8

Moving On from Guilt

The most daunting obstacle to progress is often the shadow of past failure. It is impossible to look forward if you're always looking backward. Here are some tips to working through guilty feelings that may be holding you back.

- **Acknowledge those feelings and recognize why they are there.** Guilt has a proper place in the Christian life and is a very normal human experience.

- **Don't let guilt become the focus of your mental life.** Once guilt becomes the focus, it gains power over you. It loses its purpose and can become mentally and emotionally crippling.

- **Ask yourself if you have really allowed yourself to confess the sin.** Sometimes secrecy can perpetuate a cycle of guilt. Tell God what you've done and how you feel. Don't worry about justifying yourself.

- **Seek help from a spiritual leader in your life.** If you have a propensity to feel guilt over everything or are unable to escape guilt once it has taken hold of your mind, get help.

- **Grant forgiveness to yourself.** Christ has forgiven you and wants you to have freedom from your sins. You must be willing to forgive yourself. Constant guilt produces self-loathing and will inhibit forward motion in your Christian walk. Face forward, toward the good things God desires for you.

—Kathy Tabris, Biola University

56

Awesome Wisdom

Submitting to God

By David Leyva III, Princeton University

*O the depth of the riches both of the wisdom and knowledge of God!
how unsearchable are his judgments, and his ways past tracing out!*
ROMANS 11:33, ASV

No matter how intelligent I think I am, there are things in the
Bible that I cannot fully explain. In Romans 9–11, Paul delves
into some heavy theology, and the more I read it, the more I
am convinced that I must submit to God's will. The passage
culminates in chapter 11, verse 33, in which Paul proclaims
the awesome wonder of God's wisdom and how far it is beyond our reaching. Sometimes we must submit and obey without understanding.

My first semester in the Princeton dorms was an unset-
tling time for me—a time when I did not glory in God's entire
plan. I was put in a room with three other guys, one with whom
I could not get along. The more I talked to him, the less I liked
him. He was antagonistic to my faith, he never hesitated to
bring his sinful lifestyle into our room, and he was extremely
messy. I knew I needed to share the gospel of Christ with him,
but he never seemed open enough for the message. I began to
dread going to my room just because I would have to deal with
him and his messiness.

That first semester, I was blessed to have a brother in Christ down the hall with whom I could share my thoughts. After weeks of complaining to him about my living situation, he asked me, "Do you love your roommate?" Inwardly I groaned. How could he ask me that? Of course, I didn't love my roommate!—though I knew I was supposed to. At the time, I found myself able to give up to God all the weighty things in the book of Romans that I did not understand, but I was unwilling to obey His simple and clear command to love my neighbor.

Loving my roommate took effort, but I immediately saw a change in our relationship. With the Lord's help, not only was I able to praise God as described in Romans 11, but also I saw the big "therefore" at the beginning of Romans 12.

College life is difficult even with the best of roommates. I praise the Lord that He humbled me enough in my freshman year to open my eyes to the joys of submitting my all to Him.

Jesus said to take up our cross and follow Him. How can a man think he is better than everyone else if he has a cross on his back?

Wisdom for the Week

DAY 1: 1 TIMOTHY 2:1-8

DAY 2: ROMANS 12:9-21

DAY 3: JAMES 3:13-18

DAY 4: 1 PETER 1:13-21

DAY 5: JOHN 13:31-34

Messy People Versus Neat People

Personality types can range from controlling to spontaneous, from frightfully cautious to recklessly adventurous, from orderly to chaotic. At their finest, these opposite individuals can bring out the best in one another. At their worst, the differences can fuel frustration, discontent and resentment. Here are some tips for living peacefully with your housekeeping opposite:

Tips for Neat People

- Help your messy roommate learn organizational skills without being bossy or judgmental.
- Provide large containers to hold the messy roommates' possessions (dirty dishes, clothes, books, papers, etc.) that are left in shared living spaces, but do not ever hide them or throw them away.
- Make a plan to share cleaning duties with messy roommates, and hold them accountable to do their part. Don't do their work for them unless they beg you for help.
- Don't get frustrated or controlling. Seek compromise.

Tips for Messy People

- Be considerate. You are driving your neat companions crazy. Make your bed and do your laundry!
- Try learning to be organized. It can be painful but liberating in its own surprising way.
- Take pride in your space. Don't let others clean up after you.
- Agree to share cleaning duties with your neat roommate. Keep your part of the agreement so that your roommate won't resent you. You may learn to like hanging up your clothes.

57

Not Your Father's Faith

Preparing Your Faith for Testing

By Lauren Haffner, Butler University

Now for a little while, if necessary, you have been grieved by various trials, so that the tested genuineness of your faith—more precious than gold that perishes though it is tested by fire—may be found to result in praise and glory and honor at the revelation of Jesus Christ. Though you have not seen him, you love him. Though you do not now see him, you believe in him and rejoice with joy that is inexpressible and filled with glory.

1 PETER 1:6-8, *ESV*

I'm studying religion and anthropology at a secular university. This means that most of the ideas that are going into my head are not praiseworthy knowledge about our Lord; they're ideas that glorify man's intellect or try to erase God altogether. My anthropology professor, for example, states unequivocally that humanity and the chimpanzee have a common ancestor, taking any glory out of God's creation of mankind. Many times, at the end of the day, I find myself desperately yearning for the Word.

When we go to college, we're no longer under our parents' roof. This freedom allows us to discover our own lifestyle, but it can also be frightening. We may find ourselves asking, "What am I really living for?" Or rather, "*Who* am I really living for?" Finding what faith means to us personally can be daunting—especially when our parents are no longer around to guide us.

Many new college students, no longer required to be involved in a church, sweep faith under the rug and decide it's easier to live for themselves for a while. But in light of what we know Christ has done for us, what should we do? Take heart? Cling to hope? Rely on the Holy Spirit to see us through?

"Easy to say," you might reply, "but I'm not even sure I believe anymore."

We must be prepared for doubts like these. The purpose of faith is to bring praise, glory and honor to Christ. How precious faith is! More precious than gold, which perishes, it is deemed by Christ to be worthy of His blood! We must recognize belief-testing times as necessary, meant to purify our faith and make it stronger and truer. Trials are what make our faith something more than a comfortable hand-me-down from our parents. Trials make our faith our own.

While at college, my own faith has been tested tremendously. In my Modern Religious Thought class, we were challenged to adopt a pluralistic mindset in which all religious beliefs (from Islam to atheism) augment one another. My teacher insisted that this view enhances Christianity. I do not agree—Jesus Christ is the essential element missing from other religions. Testing myself and searching out why my faith that Christ is the only way (as He says He is) was an integral part of making my faith purer and stronger than gold. Daily trials force me to turn over the dry, untouched ground of my beliefs and to cultivate a living faith in its place.

A tested, active, questioning faith has its foundation in Christ. Prepare yourself for this testing and welcome it!

Wisdom for the Week

DAY 1: LUKE 8:22-25
DAY 2: JOHN 20:34-41
DAY 3: HEBREWS 11:24-40
DAY 4: ROMANS 10:1-11
DAY 5: ROMANS 5:1-11

Creative Ways to Liven up Your Faith

We're often advised to read our Bibles and pray daily, but it's also important to realize that we can commune with God outside of the conventional quiet time.

- **Take a walk to begin or end your day.** Getting out of your dorm room and moving around may help clear your head and make room for meditation.

- **Open yourself up to conversation with those around you.** Treat every conversation as an opportunity to be encouraged, uplifted or even challenged.

- **Recognize that talking to God is a conversation.** Move away from asking prayers and really *talk* to God. Tell Him what you think and feel. Don't edit.

- **Do something you enjoy.** Let the activity itself and your enjoyment of it be a spiritual expression.

Of course, there is no formula for daily faith. Take some time to understand what will help you keep your faith alive, however unconventional the activity may seem.

—Kathy Tabris, Biola University

58

Comfort in Community

Surrounded by God's Sons and Daughters

By Kevin O'Herin, Harvard University

Carry each other's burdens, and in this way you will
fulfill the law of Christ.
GALATIANS 6:2

As my spring finals in my freshman year at Harvard were getting underway, I got a call from my parents that brought my world to a screeching halt. A family friend had committed suicide; and to make things worse, my next-door neighbor and friend, who seemed healthy the last time I saw him, was on his deathbed. The days that followed were a dark time of struggling with God. Questions I had never dealt with before brought me to my knees in grief and despair. Yet in the midst of this darkness, God's love shone brilliantly through His people's compassion.

When I first arrived at Harvard, I was confused about why God had brought me to the Ivy League school. I was unsure what challenges college would bring, and I felt very alone, far from my friends and family in Southern California. Yet I was grateful for my anchor in God, which guided my search for community. Soon I was a functioning part of the Body of Christ, both through campus fellowships and a local church.

During that time of grief and challenge, these new Christian friends comforted me as I wept. Believers I didn't even know sent emails telling me they were praying for me, for my neighbor and his family, and for the widow of the man who had killed himself. When I decided to send a last letter to my dying neighbor, dozens of friends sent along their own notes of encouragement and hope. One Sunday I broke down in church, and they stopped the service to come around me in prayer. One dear brother even offered to pay for airfare so that I could fly back to see my neighbor one last time.

I do not know how I could have endured those weeks on my own. Through that experience, God taught me that interdependence is much better than independence. He intends for us to live in community for our own sakes, and He uses our fellow Christians as conduits of His love. He is the vine, and we are the branches; apart from Him we can do nothing (see John 15:5). Often God ministers His sustaining grace to us through the sons and daughters He places around us.

Praise God for the grace He lavishes on us as we seek to be His people wherever He calls us!

Wisdom for the Week

DAY 1: PSALM 55:16-23

DAY 2: LUKE 10:30-37

DAY 3: 1 CORINTHIANS 12:14-26

DAY 4: PSALM 103:1-19

DAY 5: PHILIPPIANS 2:19-30

Finding Community

A number of national organizations offer opportunities for ministry, outreach, support and connection for Christian students. If you're yearning to find some fellow believers or you're seeking ministry opportunities, look for one of these organizations on your campus or a campus near you:

- Campus Crusade for Christ International (www.ccci.org) currently sponsors groups on more than 1,000 campus locations.

- Athletes in Action (www.aia.com) sponsors activities and outreach by and for athletic groups and fans.

- Military Campus Ministry (valor.milmin.com) is a Campus Crusade ministry that offers support for those training for military service.

- InterVarsity Christian Fellowship/USA (www.intervarsity.org) has local chapters on 560 campuses nationwide. They also have outreach groups to support graduate students and faculty, and Greek organizations.

- Student Soul (www.intervarsity.org/studentsoul) is an InterVarsity site that offers "conversation about lively faith, real relationships and life on a college campus."

- The Navigators (www.navigators.org) have organized sites on more than 170 campuses. They also host six regional conferences each year.

59

Cold

Recovering from Date Rape

[Author and University Names Withheld]

> *The LORD is close to the brokenhearted and saves*
> *those who are crushed in spirit.*
>
> PSALM 34:18

I stared at my reflection in the deserted residence-hall community bathroom and hardly recognized myself. The girl in the mirror looked so peaceful and innocent—not a hair out of place. What about the girl inside, raging against my chest? I splashed cold water on my numb face and tried to understand my evening. It had started so innocently: Two of my friends—I'll call them Max and Kyle—had invited me out for some time away from the book work; and after dinner in the cafeteria, they picked me up in their car. What could be more harmless than a get-together at their friend's place in the valley?

I trusted Max and Kyle—especially Max, whom I'd known since junior high. I thought the two of us had formed a bond for life. Yet they took me up to their place that evening, handed me an open can of soda, and the next thing I knew, I woke up half-naked in a bed.

The memory made me shudder. I turned from the mirror and staggered into the nearest shower stall and stood under the freezing water fully dressed.

Max, Kyle and my ex-boyfriend, as it turned out, had planned it all so carefully . . . and I had been a trusting fool. How could a girl who had grown up in church—a golden child, beloved by pastors and parents—tell everyone that she'd been . . . I stood there, cold water drenching me. Surely there was a better word, I hoped, than "rape"?

That night, I managed to gather my wits and slip back into my room unnoticed.

For the next five months, I kept my friends and family in the dark. It wasn't until a good friend became vaguely aware that I was holding on to some dark secret and asked me if I was okay that I blurted out the truth.

Through the healing love of my friends, my family and—most of all—my Savior, I eventually found peace with what had happened to me. There are still those moments when I ache or cry out in misery, but I am making my slow way back to becoming the happy and innocent young woman I was.

As the four-year anniversary of that night approaches, I can lift my head, look in the mirror and see a soon-to-be college graduate who is peaceful, filled with joy and bursting with love.

Wisdom for the Week

DAY 1: PSALM 34:11-22

DAY 2: PSALM 147:1-11

DAY 3: 1 PETER 1:7-11

DAY 4: MATTHEW 11:28-30

DAY 5: PSALM 145:14-21

Date Rape

Date rape is any incident of forced sex with a person you know. In some cases, alcohol or date-rape drugs render the victim unconscious or otherwise unable to resist.

Ways to Help a Victim

- *Listen.* Let the student relate her difficult experience. Assure her that you believe her story.
- *Stay calm.* Expect the victim to express a range of feelings from tears and anger to guilt and fear. Let her express her emotions without becoming emotional yourself.
- *Offer consolation rather than asking questions.* Don't offer judgment or blame.
- *Support the victim's efforts to seek help.* Encourage her to contact a campus health center for medical assistance, a local rape hotline, a student services representative, the campus safety department or local police.

Ways to Avoid Becoming a Victim

- *Go out in groups.* If you do go out alone, let a roommate or friend know where you are going, with whom and what time you plan to return.
- *Trust your instincts.* If a person, location or situation makes you feel uncomfortable, make a quick exit or call a trusted friend for help.
- *Be vigilant.* Don't accept any drink in an open container. Don't leave your own drink unattended. Know the signs and symptoms of date-rape drugs: dizziness or nausea, memory loss, blurred vision, difficulty moving or breathing, and appearing extremely intoxicated. If you or a friend experiences any of these symptoms, see a doctor and notify law enforcement as soon as possible.

Haydn No Longer

Reaching Beyond My Crowd

By Matthew Lee Scollin, Michigan State University

If you love those who love you, what credit is that to you?
Even "sinners" love those who love them. But love your enemies, do
good to them, and lend to them without expecting to get anything back.
Then your reward will be great, and you will be sons of the Most High,
because he is kind to the ungrateful and wicked.

LUKE 6:32,35

I am a music major at Michigan State University. During my freshman year, I ate, studied and hung out almost exclusively with other musicians. I even lived in West Circle, the "artsy" part of campus. All of these factors contributed to my adopting an attitude of aloofness toward the other 99 percent of the campus; as far as I was concerned, different groups of people— athletes, engineers and partyers, to name a few—were too unlike me for a meaningful relationship.

Fortunately, at the beginning of my second semester God began to whittle away at my cold exterior. I remember a specific week in which my prideful, unloving attitude became increasingly evident. And as always, God's timing was perfect: That week we had a Bible study on love.

A passage that convicted me was Romans 9:3: "For I could wish that I myself were accursed and cut off from Christ for the sake of my brothers, my kinsmen according to the flesh" (*ESV*). Paul loved the Romans so much that he was willing to sacrifice his salvation for them! Was I willing to suffer for the other 99 percent of the campus? The answer was no. God showed me that, like the Pharisees, I didn't love my neighbors—namely, the 39,900 non-music-majors at MSU—as myself.

I started to pray for God to erase my pride and help me love people as He loves them. I asked for opportunities to demonstrate Christ's love to people who were different from me. Not long afterward, I was offered a residence advisor position in South Complex, the part of campus where all the athletes live.

This presented two possibilities: Either I stayed in my West Circle comfort box with the music majors, or I trusted God and moved to South Complex, actively working on loving people who were very different from me. Through God's prompting, I chose the latter.

I'm finding that college solidifies what we hold most dear. Swallowing my pride and making the love of Christ foremost in my life has strengthened my relationship with God and others. In the end, after all, everything comes down to love—the love that nailed God's Son to a cross for our sake, and the love that continues to transform me today.

Father, thank You so much for loving me
enough to send Your Son to die for me.
Help me to show this love to others so that You
might be glorified. Amen.

Wisdom for the Week

DAY 1: MATTHEW 22:37-40

DAY 2: 1 PETER 5:5-11

DAY 3: PROVERBS 17:17-22

DAY 4: 1 THESSALONIANS 4:7-12

DAY 5: MATTHEW 5:38-48

Where Do I Belong?

Sometimes living things can thrive in unexpected circumstances. Thousands of miles from Antarctica, the Galapagos penguin makes its home in the perfect vacationing climate of the equator. While temperatures in Antarctica can drop to over 100 degrees below zero, the Galapagos Islands have a temperate 70-degree climate. The Galapagos penguin spends most of its days swimming and hunting in the island's cool waters. Though it may seem strange to picture a penguin bathing on a beach, the Galapagos penguin has adapted to and is well suited to this surprising climate.

It's important to branch out beyond what comes naturally to us, and to test our ability to adapt. This could mean making friends with people we wouldn't expect to get along with, trying something we might not be good at, or engaging with a culture outside our own. Though scary at first, challenging ourselves with the unfamiliar brings growth and eliminates the isolation that comes from pride and fear of the unknown.

—Kathy Tabris, Biola University

About the Student Authors

Ashley Akins (Azusa Pacific University)
Ashley is pursuing a bachelor's degree in social work. A Bay Area native, she is learning to love Southern California, but she left her heart in San Francisco. She is learning to love people to the best of her God-given ability, and it is her prayer that she may live each moment as if it is a gift from God.

Jeff Arnold (Biola University)
Jeff is a former college basketball player known as a "gentle giant." He stands at 6 feet 8 inches, yet he prefers writing a romantic poem to a good workout. He is an English major who plans to become a high school teacher, but he also has aspirations to write fiction someday.

Jesse Ataide (Point Loma Nazarene University)
Jesse is a devoted literature major. His favorite hangouts are the library or the local coffee house—he's the one in the corner buried under that stack of books.

Annalyse Lynn Baziuk (Sonoma State University)
Annie, a creative writing major, loves inventing stories for her little cousins and satires for her friends. She usually has some fantasy novel with her but spends her free time volunteering at the AWANA club at her church and serving as president of the SSU Fencing Club. *En garde!*

Emily E. Bennett (Biola University)
Emily is a rough-around-the-edges nursing major who loves camping, backpacking, fishing and exploring. Emily hopes to

use nursing for missions with indigenous groups or to serve the terminally ill. She writes exceptionally well with her toes and memorizes the words to almost every country song she hears.

Keena Betta (Wellesley College)

Keena, an art history and psychology major, has experienced amazing community with a very diverse group of Christian women. She hopes to go into family therapy/social work and also to be an informed museum-goer! A true California girl, she heads to the beach with friends whenever she can. She is 16 and 18 years older than her cuddly siblings, and she never misses an opportunity to incorporate rainbow sprinkles into her meals.

Hannah Bishop (Biola University)

Hannah loves the small-town life of Washington State. She's enthusiastic, opinionated and open to changing her mind.

Kim Brokate (Biola University)

Kimberly is an intercultural studies major with a passion for dance. Driven to live proactively, she spent a year living, loving and learning in Guatemala, Central America.

Matthew Castle (Azusa Pacific University)

Matt is an international business and theology double major who is trying to figure out what in the world he is supposed to do with the tremendous blessings he has been given. He loves his parents, and he isn't embarrassed to say he's afraid of grasshoppers.

Davina Choy (Biola University)

Davina, the classic English major, enjoys reading and writing. She yearns to travel across Europe and dreams of writing a novel that can move people to tears.

William Crawford (Biola University)

Will is a film production major. Proud of his homeschooling, he spent eight years studying karate but now is vice president of the campus fencing club.

John David (Azusa Pacific University)

John, a marketing major, is a washed-up jock who can still run the 40 in 4.9. He gave up football for scholastics but loves intramural competition. He's learned to be choosy about the company he keeps. Corporate America awaits him after graduation.

Anne Davis (University of Minnesota, Twin Cities)

Anne is a South Dakotan who dreams of living near some mountains or the ocean. She loves loud music, pampering her golden retriever and experiencing the outdoors. She is studying business and Spanish. Her favorite season is spring, and her major is supply chain management.

Paul DeGoes (The Master's College)

Paul is a Bible major who's also studying philosophy. When he's not browsing through impossibly dull reading material, you'll find him pumping it up in the gym, hiking local trails or swinging on the dance floor. In his own words, "Life's not about things; it's about relationships."

Schuyler Ejay Eastin, Jr. (Point Loma Nazarene University)

Schuyler is a literature major, enamoured with the written word. While he has not chosen his exact profession yet, he hopes to make writing his career.

Anya Eckelbarger (Anderson University)

Anya, a Bible and writing major, loves to travel and hang with friends until the wee hours. She's a seasoned photographer who organizes her closet by color, can't live without a filing cabinet and collects classic books.

Karen Elledge (Azusa Pacific University)

Karen hopes that her passion for painting and sculpting will lead her eventually into a career as a full-time artist. She also enjoys playing sports, watching movies and listening to music.

Mary Eriksson (Point Loma Nazarene University)

Mary Eriksson has taken flight from her undergraduate experience in Southern California. She seeks God's peace and guidance on her new life adventure.

James G. Finney (Dartmouth College)

James, a cognitive science major, grew up in Kingston, New Hampshire, and took a few years off to travel and work before college. He attended Hebrew University of Jerusalem for a short while and worked on a gubernatorial campaign. He married Sarah in October 2006; the couple looks forward to sharing a life of adventure.

Amber Kay Friudenburg (University of Texas, Austin)

Amber Kay lives in Texas. She is involved in campus ministry at the university. She is facing her fears and living by faith.

Lauren Haffner (Butler University)

Born and raised in Indiana, Lauren comes from a very loving family. She practically grew up outside, and she hasn't lost her adventurous spirit. She would love to be a traveling missionary in a few years, so she's studying religion and anthropology. Crazy fact: Lauren has a thing for books; she even loves to smell them!

Cassidy Hall (Iowa State University)

Cassidy is a liberal arts and science major who loves travel, basketball and great nonfiction books. She serves as student manager for Iowa State's women's basketball team and aspires to be a coach, to write a book and to live overseas forever, in no particular order.

Candice Hansard (Biola University)

Candice, a communication major, wants to teach English as a second language in developing countries. Since she was born and raised in the California high desert, she enjoys reading a good book in the sun. To avoid writing that big paper, she goes swing dancing or listens to Broadway musical soundtracks.

Jennifer Hare (University of California, San Diego)

Jennifer enjoys greedy shell-collecting at the beach, dabbling in poetry and photography, and anything French. She is most happy when her fingers are stained purple from berry picking or when she has a cat on her lap. Her main ambition is to grow, listen and encourage others to reach their full potential in God's love. Her majors are literature and creative writing.

Jeff Hill (Biola University)

Jeff, a journalism major as an undergraduate, loves sports and cars. He is pursuing graduate studies in student affairs so that he can work with college students for the rest of his life.

Ryan Horner (Point Loma Nazarene University)

Ryan, a literature major, has ambitions to write the Great American Novel—if he could only devise a good plot. He loves to travel and, like William Butler Yeats, forever hears "lake water lapping . . . in the deep heart's core" ("The Lake Isle of Innisfree," lines 10-12).

Brooke James (Biola University)

Brooke is a business marketing major who loves traveling, Latin culture, speaking Spanish, going to the beach, and hanging out and praying with friends. She plans to conduct international business in closed countries in hopes of bringing the Good News of Christ to those who have never heard His name.

Kobi Johnson (Abilene Christian University)

Kobi studied in Texas and now resides in Colorado. She is interested in missions work and seeks to serve Jesus.

Kara Kennedy (Point Loma Nazarene University)

Kara is pursuing a literature major and a women's studies minor. She enjoys reading science fiction and fantasy books and wants to write a book of her own someday. The best and worst part of college has been discovering more about her inner psyche.

David Leyva, III (Princeton University)

A freshman from Medford, Oregon, David is interested in American history and Spanish. Besides being involved with Christian groups on campus, he is an avid yo-yoer, juggler and T-shirt wearer. His passions for God, people and community motivate him to pursue a career in law as a judge. His academic concentration is politics.

Melissa Lilley (Campbell University)

Melissa is a mass communication major who loves watching college basketball and classic Christmas cartoon specials on television. She is editor of the university newspaper and is thankful for reruns of *The Andy Griffith Show*.

Cate McCrory (Seattle Pacific University)

Cate is a pastor's kid who has grown up hearing embarrassing stories about herself told as sermon illustrations. She loves music and sings at every opportunity.

Kylie McCuen (University of California, Santa Barbara)

Kylie is an English major who loves modern novels and Shakespeare. When she is not reading, she runs track for the Gauchos (an activity that takes up most of her time), works and tries to surf. She loves the outdoors and Santa Barbara sunsets.

Jen Montzingo (Seattle Pacific University)

Jen, a double major in elementary education and communication, now finds herself in full-time ministry at First Free Methodist Church. She's crazy about making shabby-chic cards, sampling Thai food with friends and wearing a good pair of gold kitten heels. After a brief stint working in film and later appearing as a reality show bachelorette, Jen's dream job is to speak and write for *Revolve: Teen Women of Faith*.

Trevor Nagle (Biola University)

Trevor, an English major, decided to become a writer after winning $300 in a fourth-grade essay contest. While the money seemed great at the time, he soon discovered it wouldn't quite cover his massive school tuition. As an English major, he is searching for a career path alongside other students who once thought they wanted to make their living as writers.

Heather A. Nelson (university name withheld)

Heather is an English major with ambitions of becoming a copy editor. Her passion is for children living in the inner city, and she hopes she can have an influence on them as they try to succeed in life. Heather delights in spending time with friends and family and continues to become the woman God made her to be.

Kevin O'Herin (Harvard University)

Kevin grew up as an MK in Germany, Russia, Finland, Australia and the United States. He is pursuing Hispanic studies. He hopes to use his life to give glory to God overseas but is still searching to figure out what that means.

Kristen Orem (Biola University)

Kristen loves daisies, the sun and the beach. The thing she hates most is being bored. She loves chick flicks, and she watches *Ever After* every night as she falls asleep.

Hannah Naomi Pizelo (Biola University)

Hannah is an enthusiastic film directing major who has loved her involvement in student government, debate, speech, dance and languages. She enjoys her family, pursuing God, sharing with close friends, and anything that requires creativity or English tea.

Katleyn Pollet (Montreat College)

Katleyn, a human services major, hopes to pursue graduate study someday. She leads a group of middle-school girls at her church and loves dancing and photography. Her roommate is now one of her best friends. She's learned that God uses trials to strengthen His children and to reveal His love.

Karen Porter (Yale University)

Karen is a history and international studies major who enjoys writing, running and world traveling. Before Yale, she spent two years at Pepperdine University, which was especially instrumental in inspiring her love for service. Someday Karen hopes to serve in international diplomacy and to write a screenplay, and in everything make a difference for Jesus!

Hillary Prag (Seattle Pacific University)

Hillary is a sociology major known for her creative and often exotic pursuits. For example, she once taught orphans in Uganda to make fabulous newspaper hats. She grew up under Colorado's mile-high sun but now lives in Seattle where she is pursuing a career in everything.

Katie Putnam (University of Georgia)

Katie enjoys good books and asking questions. She loves to laugh at corny jokes and squirrels, and in her spare time she can often be found obsessively watching the Food Network. Above all else, she desires to passionately pursue God.

Hilary Reddick (Michigan State University)

Hilary is studying music education. She wants to be a middle-school choir teacher because she believes that music speaks to people's spirits in a unique way that God can use for His glory. God has blessed her with an amazing Christian family, and He continues to show her the blessings we have in the Body of Christ.

Leah Danielle Robin (Whitworth College)

Leah gets around campus on her long board. She's studied ballet, dabbled in intramural Frisbee competitions and loves her students in the New Community Youth Group. An English major who enjoys writing for her college newspaper, *The Whitworthian,* she hopes to be the editor of her own magazine one day.

Jennette Rogers (Anderson University)

Jennette studies English, writing and flute performance. She loves to travel. Her favorite destination thus far is England, where she spent two glorious weeks in 2005. She also likes shopping and scrapbooking in her spare time.

Matthew Lee Scollin (Michigan State University)

Matthew is studying vocal music performance. He grew up in Walled Lake, Michigan, with his mom. He loves Jesus, his family and music; everything he is comes as a result of those loves. Lord willing, he plans to pursue a career as an opera singer.

Sarah Schwartzendruber Shaffer (Taylor University)

Sarah has a degree in English and loves books too much. She never finds enough time to tackle her ever-growing list of books to read because she's always cooking, baking, taking long walks or watching great movies.

Alicia Shocki (Montreat College)

Alicia, a Washington native, plays college softball. She hopes to pursue a graduate degree in entertainment law to eventually work in the record industry. Her favorite authors are C. S. Lewis, J. D. Salinger and George Orwell.

Ryan Simmons (Cedarville University)

Ryan, an English major, enjoys reading and writing but avoids grammatical topics at all costs. On any warm sunny day, you'll often find him hiking local trails, enjoying his rural roots.

Ryan Smernoff (Biola University)

Ryan loves friends, adventures and philosophy tomes. In high school, he was named Most Spontaneous and Biggest Klutz, and both titles still apply. He aspires to be a professor of philosophy.

Naomi Spurrier Smith (Houghton College)

Some of Naomi's favorite things include Christmas music, fresh air and warm cups of tea on cold days. After confusing her classmates by entering college with her twin sister, Rachel, she majored in English literature and studied abroad for two splendid semesters in London, England.

Angela Story (Southeastern University)

Angela enjoys playing the piano and devouring chocolate. An aspiring English teacher, she loves reading good books and sharing them with others.

Sara Van Valkenburg (Biola University)

Sara, a history major from Colorado, loves mountains and spending time around a campfire. When inside, she curls up with a favorite blanket to read children's novels. To keep herself safe, she watches cop movies and then practices self-defense moves on her friends.

Megan Wilhelm (Spring Arbor University)

Megan is an English major who loves reading, scrapbooking and exploring her family tree. For her, a relaxing evening includes a comfy chair, a Christian romance novel and a cup of peppermint tea.

Matthew Williams (Biola University)

Matt is an English major who enjoys all music (as long as it's not country) and all sports. He was a two-time all-league football player in high school and is currently the captain of his college lacrosse team.

Elizabeth Kay York (Whitworth College)

Elizabeth, a Texan, knew she wanted to be a writer by age eight and now contributes articles to her local newspaper, *The Odessa American*. She loves her Tuesday-night Latin and ballroom dance class and her Thursday-night Bible study. She hopes to return to Irish dance class if she ever finds the time.

Acknowledgments

Many thanks are due to our colleagues at various universities who helped us make contact with many of our contributors, especially Carol Blessing, Thomas Mannarino, Sandie Holt and Steve Rugg; to friends and family who helped flesh these pages out, especially Heather Buchanan, Todd Miller, Shannon Kooistra and Kathy Tabris; to our spouses, Gary and Revy, for allowing us to clutter up our kitchen tables with so many folders and papers; and to all the student contributors from around the country who made this compilation possible.

More Great Resources from Regal

Writing on the Wall
Prayers, Psalms and Laments
of the Rising Culture
Brian Heasley
ISBN 978.08307.43674

Fearless
Reflections on Fear
*Tom Stephen &
Virginia Starkey*
ISBN 978.08307.42950

**The 10 Most Common
Objections to Christianity**
Alex McFarland
ISBN 978.08307.42981

Punk Monk
New Monasticism and the
Ancient Art of Breathing
Andy Freeman & Pete Greig
ISBN 978.08307.43681

Available at Bookstores Everywhere!

Visit **www.regalbooks.com** to join **Regal's FREE e-newsletter.**
You'll get useful **excerpts** from our newest releases and **special
access to online chats** with your favorite authors. Sign up today!

Regal
God's Word for Your World™
www.regalbooks.com